# JOURNEY TO THE UNSEEN WORLD

by
Ayatullah Najafi Quchani

# 1
## Chapter

## FOREWORD

Man instinctively desires to have an understanding of the life Hereafter, i.e. the life after death and the state of the Barzakh (the interval between death and resurrection), which we all have to face.

Knowledge of "Barzakh" is required because Barzakh is completely different from this world. So, man wishes to know how his present lifestyle and his activities here will affect his life in the Barzakh. Certain questions rise in his mind, like: what sort of people will he encounter there? What kind of beings live there? Do eating, drinking, sleeping, waking friendship, enmity etc, exist there, and if so in what form? What is the span of time between death and resurrection (Barzakh) and what will his activities be in this period? What do happiness and wretchedness in Barzakh entail?

Principally, does a spirit need a body after death or does it become permanently free and independent of the body and becomes engaged in an infinite journey towards an unknown destination? Whether the spirits will be granted bodies and if so, will these bear any resemblance to our present bodies? And whether the spirits are able to communicate with the people living on earth or do communication and contact stop forever?

This book attempts to answer these and other similar questions. The late author has attempted to take his reader on a tour of the Barzakh and the land of the spirits. For some time he takes man away from the base and material, away from the noise and hustle of the world, and into the very lap of the spiritual and angelic state, that is, the life in the Barzakh.

Principally speaking, Man with his limited senses and knowledge is unable to understand or even correctly perceive the state of life in Barzakh, as he does not have any knowledge about the state of affairs there. Man's senses are so weak, that even in this world, which is so small compared to the universe, one is a prisoner of time and space and he is incapable of looking into the future.

Life after death, is of course, a specially difficult topic. To analyse, understand and then explain in simple language is next to impossible. This is because man has only experienced a life which is very limited; in comparison, Barzakh is infinite and unlimited. Apart from this, the events which will take place after death are those which are yet to occur; and man's knowledge and information are always based on past events which have already occurred. Hence how can man have knowledge of a thing which he is yet to experience?

If this is the case. then is the path to awareness and knowledge completely closed, and should man, therefore, abandon all his attempts to seek out the truth?

But it is not so. God has given man a way out. The sole means which can help man are the revelations and scriptures or the Holy Books, and side by side those pious and holy personalities whom are commonly called Prophets and their true successors. These are the only sources of illumination and guidance which man has to take him out of the narrow straits of darkness, ignorance and bewilderment. The lives of the Prophets and their successors were free from all tainments. They were the Truthfuls, the Witnesses. They were certainly neither frauds and liars, nor simpletons and fantasizing men who, either out of greed or ignorance, created fantasies and presented them to men. On the contrary, on the basis of their wisdom, knowledge of facts and their in-depth understanding, and also as being a source of peace and blessing for entire mankind, they should be considered as the best amongst the human race. Many of their sayings appear strange and even wrong but are in fact right. This is because their knowledge stems from the fountain of revelation and the Holy Books, and these are free of error and doubt. God has revealed these books of guidance and light to wipe out ignorance and for awakening of mankind. The best, most complete and perfect of these books is the Holy Qur'an. Similarly, amongst the righteous guides, the Holy Prophet stands out as the best and most perfect, followed by his successors.

The gist of the Qur'an and the teachings of the Ahl ul bait is that our life in this world is very short and untrustworthy and that life after death exists, it is a reality and it is eternal. The fortunate in this world is the one who leads a life of faith, awareness and awakening and in accordance with the commandments of God. In the Hereafter, he will lead a life of eternal happiness and will be rewarded with boundless blessings. And the one who leads a life of neglectfulness, waywardness and evil doings, for him there will be eternal punishment and chastisement.

Doubtless, the Hereafter encompasses an infinite life-span

and our life in this world, even if we attain an age of 70, 80 or even 100 years, in comparison with the Hereafter, is merely like a drop of water compared to the sea. How ignorant and unjust is then indeed man, to give so much time and importance to his worldly pleasures and become so forgetful of his next life!

This book attempts to draw a picture of the Barzakh in the light of the Qur'an and the traditions of the Prophet and his successors. It shows the bliss of the virtuous and the wretchedness of the evil-doers, with the help of examples and hints taken from the verses and the traditions.

It is hoped that readers and esteemed scholars will overlook and forego any mistakes which may be present.

# 2
Chapter

## THE STATION OF THE GRAVE AND THE BEGINNING OF BARZAKH WESTWARD TRAVEL

In the name of Allah, the Benevolent and Ever Merciful

All Praise belongs to Allah, the Lord of the Universe, the Master of this world and of the Day of Judgment.

Peace and blessings be on the Prophet of Islam and on his Progeny who warned us that love of this world is a dangerous affliction and that it is the root cause of all diseases afflicting the human race. All other diseases are really branches stemming from this main root. And the cure of this affliction is to keep reminding oneself constantly of Death.

I begin now, by saying that, in 1307 H I had written my memories about my schooling and had called it Travel Eastwards. And now in 1312 when I am writing about the Barzakh, I intend to call it Westward Travel and I hope that it will serve as a souvenir from me and will prove a source of guidance and advice for the general public.

The fact is that our present material and elemental body, by virtue of its very nature, is in a dark and impenetrable veil, not allowing man to see into any other world. Death, in fact, is the name of emerging from this curtain and once this curtain is removed, man is able to see that which was hidden to his eyes before, and he becomes aware of facts which he was unaware of, until then.

'Certainly, you were heedless of this (day), now we have removed your veil from you, so now your sight is sharp'. (Surah Qaf Verse 22)

That is to say, in this world you were ignorant of facts. Now after death we have removed from your eyes the material curtain so that you may clearly see the Hereafter.

Hence, I died. Then I saw myself standing, relieved of my illness, feeling fit and healthy, but around my corpse my relatives were busy mourning. I was saddened by their crying and told them that I was cured and not dead but nobody heard me.

It was as if they neither saw nor heard me.[1] I realized that these people had now become distant from me and so I turned my complete attention towards my corpse. I became especially attentive towards the face and the side, which was uncovered. Afterwards, my body was bathed and shrouded. Then, when the people had taken care of their other pending work, they took my body towards the graveyard. I was also present in the funeral procession. In this procession I saw many wild beasts and animals, which frightened me, but the other people present were neither afraid nor even troubled, as if those beasts were their tame and beloved pets. In this way, we reached the graveyard. I

---

[1] (Kitab-e-Manazil-eAkhirat by Mohaddise Oummi)

stood in the grave, and saw how my body was lowered into it, head first. The moment the body was laid inside, the grave became full of animals emerging from everywhere.

My fear knew no bounds especially when the animals started attacking my body. But the man who was lowering my body was not in the least fearful, it was as if he did not even see them.

The man laid the body in the grave and then came out. But my primary interest was in my body so I stayed inside the grave. I tried to shy away the animals but they were too many for me to handle and they overcame me. One reason was that I was so overcome with fear that my very existence was trembling. I called out to the people standing above my grave for help but nobody came forward to help. On the contrary they remained busy in their work, as if they just could not see the commotion that was going on inside the grave. Suddenly certain people entered the grave from somewhere and came to my help, as the animals ran away when they saw these people. So I thanked them and asked them who they were that they had helped me in such a difficult time. They smiled and replied that they were my good deeds that I had done and that the beasts had been my evil deeds. They asked me if I had not heard the verse "Verily the good deeds clear away the bad deeds". Then these people disappeared.

As soon as the commotion was over, I regained my senses. I saw that the men outside had closed the grave and had left me alone in the dark and narrow place. I could see the people going back to their houses, even my close friends, relatives and family members had deserted me and left me alone. These were the very people for whose comfort and well being I had provided and worked for day and night. Their desertion and unfaithfulness on the one hand and my dark and narrow prison on the other extremely saddened me and I was close to bursting with sorrow.

I had never before felt such fear and bewilderment and I sat down dejected at the head of the corpse, losing all hopes of receiving any help from anybody except God. I was wondering what would happen next, when suddenly the grave started trembling and dust came falling down off its walls and roof. It was especially violent near the foot of the grave as if some huge beast was trying to split open the grave to enter. Finally the grave did split and two huge men with fearful faces entered.[(2)]

The two men were strong and hefty like giants. Smoke and fire bellowed from their mouths and nostrils. In their hands were iron rods so red not that it seemed as if flames were leaping up from them. Suddenly they thundered in voices so sharp that the heavens and earth trembled, "Who is your Lord?"

I was so afraid that I could not control my senses. I lost the power to speak and my courage gave way. I thought my dead body would not be able to answer their questions and I became certain that they would give the body a good beating with their iron rods and the grave would be engulfed with fire. I saw that as it were their fear had made me lose control over my senses, if fire engulfed the grave it would become much worse. So I decided to answer their questions myself. I beseeched God for help: "O Helper of the Helpless and Rescuer of the Troubled and Afflicted, come to my help. In my heart I also seek the intercession of Imam Ali because I knew him well and I was aware of his strength, and of his position in the eyes of God and that he could come to one's help at any place and at all times. I believed him to be the dispenser of difficulties. My heart had been full of love for him throughout my life and even in death. I knew that this intercessor was God's blessing and that in the most difficult of times when man is near to losing his senses, this gift of God comes to his rescue.

The Qur'an says, "And you see men in stupor, and they are not in stupor, but God's chastisement is severe" (Sura Hajj verse 2). But even in such times, the Imam comes to help. Hence as soon as I seek his intercession, in spite of the gravity of the situation, strength returned to me and I felt capable of answering.[3]

But my lengthy silence had angered them all the more. Their flaming eyes and faces became harsher. They raised their arms as if about to strike me with their iron rods and in voices sharper than before they repeated, "Who is your Lord?"

But I was no longer afraid and so I replied softly that Allah, the One, Only and Unique was my Lord. "He is Allah; there is no God but he, the knower of the unseen and the seen, He is the Beneficent and Ever Merciful. He is Allah, there is no God but He, the King, the Holy, the Peace-loving, the Bestower of conviction, the Guardian, the Ever-prevalent, the supreme, the great absolute. For too exalted is Allah from what they associate (with him). (Soora Hashr verse 22, 23)

I remembered this particular verse because I had been in the habit of reciting it daily after my morning prayers.[4]

I felt it necessary to recite it in front of them in order to convince them of my position and qualities, so that they may not think that the human race was bereft of lofty qualities. They had objected to the creation of Adam the very first day saying that he would prove to be naught but a source of mischief and bloodshed on earth. However, I saw that as soon as I recited these verses, their anger seemed to melt away. Their faces softened somewhat and one of them told the other that it seemed as if I belonged to the group of scholars of Islam and therefore they should continue with their questioning in a gentler manner.

But the other one replied that God had appointed them to question me and so they should continue in the same manner regardless of who I was. Because their attitude towards me should depend only upon my being able to answer correctly all the questions and it was not yet known whether l would be able to do so.

After conversing thus, they resumed their questioning, "Who is your Prophet?"

But now I felt sufficiently courageous and, even my voice was strong. Without hesitation I replied, "The Messenger and the Prophet of God towards all men, Muhammad, the son of Abdullah, May Peace be Upon Him and his progeny. He is the seal of the Messengers and the head of the Prophets. The moment I replied, their anger vanished completely and their faces brightened and became happy. Then they questioned me about my Book, Temple, and the Imams and the successors of the Holy Prophet. I replied, "My book is the Holy Qur'an, which was revealed by the benevolent Lord unto the sagacious Prophet (S.A.). And my temple is the Kaaba and the Masjid-ul-Haraam 'wherever you maybe, turn your faces towards it' and 'I have turned my face towards the Creator of the heavens and the earth completely and submissively and I am not from the polytheists'. And my Imams and the successors of the Holy Prophet are the Twelve Imams, the first of them Ali, and the last Imam Mehdi, who is the Imam and the ruler of our time. Obedience unto them is obligatory and they are infallible. They are the Witnesses on the earth and in the

Hereafter they are the intercessors." Then I named each Imam with his parentage and other details.

To this they replied that such a lengthy discourse was unnecessary and the answers should be brief. I promptly remarked "This detail was necessary for you because you had misgivings about the creation of Adam from the very first day. Your objection to the creation of Adam had in fact been an objection on the action of God. And from the day that I understood your objection, it was like a burden on me. And I had promised myself that whenever I would meet you, I would question you thoroughly; but it is sad that now when we have met, the situation does not permit it: I am in a difficult position and you have been appointed by God to question me."

Then I fell silent and waited to see their reaction. But they stopped their interrogation and merely asked me the source of these answers. This question was a source of concern and worry because I thought that the proofs and theories that I had prepared in the world concerning the Beliefs and principles of Islam, were they indeed necessarily true? The possibility existed that even Aristotle, who's considered to be the Father of Philosophy, was wrong. In fact, some of his fallacies were in my notice. Secondly, those proofs even if correct would hold true only in the dark and ignorant world, whereas here was a world of Light and Illumination. Darkness necessitates a guiding stick but here the darkness had gone and was replaced with light of such luminance that even the blind would not require a guiding stick. Of what use was the stick (my proof) now? Then what did these two, want from me? "O God! I am a newcomer here and I am yet unaware of the prevalent customs and of the nature of the beings present here. O God! I beseech you in the name of Imam Ali, the son of Abu Talib, help me!"

I was thus engrossed in my thoughts and supplications. When suddenly their piercing scream, sharper than flint, rang out. 'Answer at once What was the source from which you learnt these answers?[5]

(5) (It is necessary to know the beliefs and principles of Islam like the Unity of God, Divine Justice, Prophethood, Imamat and the Day of Judgement, through understanding and logical proof. In this case, Taqleed following a Marjaa or scholar is not permitted. It is not sufficient if one adopts these beliefs because his forefathers believed in them. Blind following in this manner will prove useless in the Hereafter. As Islam is a religion of logic and evidence, the Muslim should strive to know the Beliefs and principles through logic and clear understanding of proofs.

If this is not done, then his beliefs cannot be considered to be free of doubt and he would consequently not qualify to stand amongst the true Muslims in the Hereafter. Faith is a state of the heart, but it is attained only when religion has been principles through logic. Otherwise, Islam obtained through mere following is not of lasting quality and does not provide the necessary incentive required to work for the Hereafter. However proper understanding of religion through logic and proofs will result in the height of awareness and knowledge, which in turn will prove to be an incentive for doing deeds for the Hereafter.

And God willing, any one who acts with sincerity and with correct principles will be rewarded in the Hereafter. However, if these essentials of correct principles, sincerity of intention, and quality and quantity of deeds are lacking, then the future can prove bleak.

I could no longer bear to look at their faces. Their eyes

were red with anger and flames were leaping up from them, their faces were terrifying. Their mouths were wide open like a lion's with fang-like teeth visible inside. Their iron rods were raised as if they were lust about to strike. Overcome with fear, I almost fainted. At this moment, the answer seemed to be revealed to me. I answered in a weak voice: "I was guided towards these words by Allah." They replied 'then sleep like the really wed pride". They went away but I felt as if I had either gone to sleep or had fainted. But I clearly felt that I was rid of the fear and I slept peacefully.

When I revived and opened my eyes, I saw myself in a pleasant room. A handsome youth, hose very body was fragrant was sitting next to me with my head in his lap, waiting for me to wake up. I sat up out of respect for him and greeted him. He smiled lovingly embraced me and returned my greetings, and said, "sit down and be at ease. I'm your friend and companion, not a Prophet or an Imam.

"I asked, "May I know who you are? It is indeed my good fortune to have a companion like you. It is my desire to always remain with you."
He replied, "My name is Haadi (Guide), I am also called Abul Wafa (the Father of fulfillment) and Abu Turab (Father of earth). I guided you to your first answer. Had you failed to reply, they would have given you a good beating with their iron rods and your grave would have become full with the flames from Hell." I replied, "'I am indeed grateful to you for your help in freeing me from the dire straits I was in but as that as I'm concerned, the last question was unnecessary and was merely in order to lengthen the questioning process. I had replied correctly to all the questions about the Islamic beliefs. And if one speaks truthfully about factual events, then there is no scope left for questioning. If you keep a red-hot iron on

somebody's palm and he complains that his hand is burning, it is superfluous to ask why he is saying so. If in spite of this a man is foolish enough to ask, then the reply can only be to ask him if he is blind that he cannot see the red-hot iron lying on the hand. The last questions which the angels asked can only be termed to be of this category."

Haadi replied, "This is not correct, because man does not usually speak the truth. It is quite possible that he admits to certain truths verbally, but in the heart of hearts he does not believe in them. If the heart does not firmly believe in a principle, it will not act in accordance to it. Such words and admissions are meaningless, as the heart does not believe in them. As God has said, 'Do not claim that you have brought faith, only say that you have submitted, faith has not yet entered your hearts.

"On the very first day when man was asked 'Am I not your Lord?' all did not reply in the affirmative and submit to God's Lordship as they should have."
I inquired "Why"?

Haadi replied, "In the material world when man is tested for his religious duties and responsibilities, many fail to observe these dutifully until the time arrives to come out of the examination hall. After death, here in the first station, the true believer and the hypocrite both answer the questions correctly until the last question is asked. If true faith had place in his heart, then only is he able to answer as you did. If, however, the foundation of his beliefs and his religion lay in traditions and customs and not in sound logic, then as deep down in his heart he does not believe in it, it proves useless here. You are aware yourself of the traditions of the Prophet and his progeny concerning this."

I replied, "That's true, the traditions of the Infallibles indeed speak of this. But the questioning terrified me so much, that I could not even think logically, and forgot all about this. May God bless you for coming to my help at such a crucial time. And I pray to God that he may never bereave me of your company.

"But first, tell me, how is it that though we've never met before, you seem to know me well, and in spite of the short time that we've been together, I've developed such a love for you that I cannot bear to part with you?"

He replied, 'I have been with you since the very first day and have always loved you but you never sensed my presence since in the material world your sight lacked the power to perceive me.

Actually, "I am the relationship of love and friendship which you had with Imam Ali and the Ahl ul bayt of the Holy Prophet. My meeting and helping a person depends upon the strength of that relationship, that is to say, it depends upon his capability. I'm called the Haadi (the guide) because the love of Ahl ul bayt guides a man towards good deeds, but only according to his capability. In other words, I was your guide as far as you are concerned and Ali is the Imam, guide and leader of all the pious people on earth. And the Holy Our'an, 'that is the Book, there is no doubt in it, it is a guidance for the pious,' this book and myself we are your guides to the extent of the connections and relations which you had with us. And 'One who disowns tempestuousness and believes in God, then verily he has taken hold of the strong rope which is not going to break, and so I am not going to part with you, unless you yourself part with me through following your carnal desires. This is why I am called Abul Wafa. The (father of Faithfulness) and Abu Turab (Father of Earth).[6]

(6) (Here the author has embodied the love of Ahl ul bayt

to show how this love will come to help in all situations. The famous tradition of the Holy Prophet says: "One who dies loving of the Progeny of Mohammed, dies a Martyr". Imam Mohammad Baqar stated to Abu Khalid kabuli. "O, Abu Khalid! By God, the love of Ahl ul bayt illuminates the heart of the faithful like the sun illuminates the day". Imam Shaafai says: "I firmly hold on to the rope (covenant) of Allah, as we have been commanded, and this is the love of Ahl ul bayt". But it should be pointed out that mere vows of love are not sufficient unless one's deeds are also in accordance. The eighth Imam, Raza (A.S.) said: "We do not have a permit to free any one from the flames of Hell. And our intercession cannot overcome Divine Justice. One who is obedient to Allah is our friend, and the one who is disobedient is our foe". This shows that a claim of love and friendship of Ahl ul bayt will hold only when backed with deeds, which are according to Ahl ul bayt's wishes and desires. Otherwise to continue leading a life bereft of good deeds and even indulge in evil and then to depend upon the love of Ahl ul bayt is to deceive oneself.)

In short, my creation is from the light of Ali (A.S.). I was present in your heart in accordance with your capability, that is, to the extent that you acted in accordance with your vows of love of Ali. I could only stay with you when you did good. When you were disobedient, I used to part with you. Similarly, here I will be with you when you are rewarded for your good deeds, but when you are punished for your evil actions, you will not find me present. Allah has stated in the Qur'an: 'This is because God does not do injustice to his people, but they do injustice to themselves.

"However, today was the last day of your life on earth and is the first day of the Hereafter. I was merely a trust of God given to you for sate keeping. What saddens me most is that you have read the Qur'an time and again and the Qur'an is full of my mention, yet today you did not even recognize me. Anyway, I'll leave now and for the present you may rest, 'God be with you."

Haadi went away leaving me alone. I started contemplating on the events and the fact dawned upon me that it was as if life in the world was a dream and man wakes up after death to find the interpretation of his dream becoming a reality.

"O Pity that I overstepped (the bounds) in the court of Allah" (Soora-eZamr verse 53) (that is, I kept sinning, without realizing God to be present and a witness to my deeds), but now it was useless to cry and feel pitiful for myself because the door of atonement and repentance was now closed. I was engulfed in these thoughts when I fell asleep. But I was soon awakened by another calamity. This time I felt two men sitting on either side; the one on the right was beautiful, but the one on left was ugly to look at. They were sniffing my body from head to toe and kept entering something in the files, which they had in their hands. They had brought along some boxes of various sizes and they kept the body like the heart, the power of thought, power of intention, were subjected time and again to their sniffing whilst they whispered amongst themselves. Repeated the sniffing procedure, filled the boxes and sealed them.

I remained still that they might not realize I was awake but I was terrified because I realized that they were judging my deeds and recording them. The good looking man seemed to be a well-wisher because from what little I could overhear it seemed as if he was not allowing those sins for which I had repented to be recorded. At times he would say that such and such sin had been compensated by a certain good deed that I had done, just as the alchemist's elixir turns earth into gold. So I developed a liking for this person because of his kindness towards me. When they finished writing, they folded the sheets and wrapped them around my neck like fetters, and they put the sealed boxes in a bag and placed it by my head. Then I saw them bringing an iron cage; it had thick iron bars and was about my size. They put me inside, and bolted it. Then, as they turned its lever, it started to constrict, tightening on my body. It became so tight that it became difficult to breath, and I felt that I could not even call to anybody for help. They kept turning the lever until the cage, which had originally been my size, was now no bigger than a small cooking vessel; small and hot. My bones cracked and broke and quite literally oil oozed out of my body, as black as soot. They mopped it up but I had fainted and was unaware of what was going on.

When I became conscious again, I found my head in Haadi's lap I said, "Haadi forgive me. But I am feeling so bad that I cannot even get up. My joints have all broken, and I cannot yet breathe properly." My voice had gone weak and I was crying as if I was reproaching Haadi for not being present when I had needed him so much. This was the first constriction that I had ever faced. Haadi consoled me and told me that what had happened to me was an unavoidable event which everyone had to face in the first stage in the grave. Anyhow, he hoped that I would not have to face similar events in the future. Secondly, he said, all events here were a result of my own past deeds.[7]

(7) (Constriction in the grave and other punishments of the Barzakh, are the result of those sins which one has not repented for. It has nothing to do with correctness of one's faith. The possibility exists that a person though a true faithful commits certain mistakes or sins in his lifetime, and will have to bear the punishment for these in the Hereafter. Therefore man should only sin to an extent that he can bear to be punished for. Saad Ibne Maaz was one of the respected companions of the Holy Prophet. When he died, the Holy Prophet accompanied his funeral bare foot and

without his cloak to show his grief. The Prophet himself laid Saad in the grave, prayed for him and said that Gabrail and Meekail along with a host of angels were present in the funeral. But when Saad's mother said, 'O Saad! You are indeed fortunate that the Holy Prophet has walked barefoot in your funeral and has lowered you in your grave, The Holy Prophet asked her to be quiet and said, You cannot prevent him from suffering the punishment of the grave. Saad did not treat his family members kindly and so is now suffering constriction.").

But the cage that you saw is created by men's own evil traits. It is possible that for some it night be thousand times more painful. There are three basic vices 1) Avarice and greed. 2) Conceit and arrogance. 3) Jealousy.

The first of these was responsible for the expulsion of Adam from heaven, the second expelled Satan from God's court and the third sent Kane headlong to Hell. From these three stem thousands of branches and depending on lack or excess of these, men possess their individual characters and traits.

Haadi kept on talking and consoling me. Simultaneously he kept moving his hands gently over my back, sides and other affected parts. And it relieved my pain and gave me renewed strength.

My body appeared to have been purged of all debasements and had become pure and clean. I now understood that the constriction had actually been an act of purifying so that if man possessed evil traits these debasements would, as a result of the constriction, be squeezed out of him like the black oil, which I had, seen.

In reply to my questioning, Haadi replied, "The big bag

contains your luggage. Open it so that I may also see what you have brought along for your journey."

I opened the bag and found inside the sealed boxes. Some of these contained an inscription that they were meant to be used at certain destinations. There were also packets of rewards and punishments containing labels that they would be opened at specific places. I asked Haadi, "What do these boxes contain?"

Haadi replied, "These are the very moments of the days and nights that you have spent in which you have done good or evil. Whenever an act was committed, the boxes opened like oysters and preserved your acts like valuable gems. These moments are now present in these boxes in front of you."

Then I asked, "What is this chain in my neck?" Haadi replied, "This is your Deed Sheet. You will be judged on its basis on the Day of Judgment. For the present (in Barzakh) it is not required. As the Qur'an says in Soora-e-Asra, verse 14, 'We have made the destiny of every human being cling to his neck and we shall bring forth for him on the Day of Resurrection a book which he will find wide open."

Then he said, "I see that you have very little provision for your life in the Eternal abode. I suggest that you stay here for a few Fridays as your friends and heirs in the world might send some gifts for you, because the Holy Prophet has said, 'The more provision you have in your journey (of Hereafter) the better it is' I will go now and, try to obtain a passport for you from the King of the World and the Hereafter. No orders have been issued in this regard in the past week. On Thursday night, I suggest you go and visit your family. Maybe they will think of you and pray for your well being and forgiveness."

Haadi left and I sat down to wait for his return. But my stay now was in a pleasant place and the room was well carpeted. Thursday night arrived but there was yet no sign of Haadi. I decided to follow his advice and in the form of a white dove. I alighted on a branch of a tree near my house on earth in order to see my family.[8]

[8] (Allama Majlisi in his book Haqqul Yaqeen writes that the spirits came to visit their family weekly, monthly, or annually depending upon their rank. They arrive in the form of a bird, and sit on the wall of the house and watch. If the family members are happy and busy in good deeds, the spirit also becomes happy and if otherwise, the spirit becomes sad. On Thursday nights, these spirits arrive. An angel accompanies the spirits of the faithful. If the family members are in any kind of hardship, then the angel shields them from the spirit's view, that he may not be troubled by their plight.)

I saw my family members but I was all the more saddened, they were doing what they considered would prove beneficial for me. My friends and relatives had gathered. Qur'an was being recited, a Majlis was being addressed, and good food had been prepared. But I could feel that all this was merely for custom's sake. The sole aim was to put up a good show. The people being served the dinner were all wealthy, and not in the least needy. Not a single poor or deprived and deserving soul was to be seen. Of what good was such food for me? One could see that even the guests had come to fulfill the customs. They were so callous that even by mistake they were not served promptly; they did not hesitate from cursing my heirs and me. My relatives were not even mourning Imam Hussain. Some were lamenting that they were now bereft of a guardian. Others were crying over the loss of their sustainer and worrying for the future. It was clear that they had no thoughts for me, and were only interested in themselves. So much so, that they were even oblivious of their own hereafter. Of what use was all this for me? It saddened me further that they seemed to be complaining as if the Master and the Creator had committed an injustice unto them; they were objecting to the actions of the Wise and All-knowing God. I lost hopes of receiving any good from this quarter and dejectedly returned to my abode. I was close to expressing my anger and displeasure with, my family, but then I realized that for them the misfortune of being separated from me was calamity enough. When I reached my grave, I found Haadi waiting inside for me. I saw a tray of ripe and fresh apples lying in the center of the room. I asked, "Where have these come from?" He replied, "Somebody passed by your grave today and recited Surah-e-Fateha for you. Since his was a sincere act, the Merciful decided that you should be promptly rewarded. May God bless him too." Then Haadi busied himself in decorating my room. He arranged the divans, sofas and the chairs, and hung ornaments on the walls. A chandelier was also fixed and its light was bright and luminescent as the sun. I said, "Haadi, you yourself said that this is not my permanent place. Then why are you taking so much pains today in decorating this room?" He replied, "I have received information that the Imam's son whose grave you had visited once, and the religious scholars whom you used to remember in your Night Prayers are coming to visit you in order to thank you for your friendship."

I replied, "This is indeed my good fortune and it compensates for the sadness that I felt after visiting my family."

I kept thinking that such good fortune was indeed more

then what a sinner like me could ever have hoped for.(9)

(9) (In Usool-e-kafi, Imam Sadiq is quoted as saying that in the west there is a beautiful garden, watered by the Furaat. The spirits of the faithful reside here. They recognize each other and visit each other. In the mornings they are free to fly out from here. In the East there is another valley, this one in meant for the wicked and the sinners. Here the spirits are punished for their past deeds, their food is bitter and their water stinks. Probably this description refers to the Valley of Peace and the Valley of Barhoot.)

I told Haadi that my room was small and not fit to accommodate such personalities. He replied that it was small for me but that when the guest would arrive, it would expand accordingly.

Suddenly the guests arrived and seated themselves according to their ranks and station. Their majestic faces shone. The most prominent of them were Hazrat Abbas and Hazrat Ali Akber. They sat down on a gold divan but I noticed that they were fully dressed for war-helmet, shield, sword etc. I wondered at the need for all this here, but I was so awestruck that I could not muster the courage to speak.

Haadi, others, and myself lined up respectfully in front of Hazrat Abbas and Hazrat Ali Akber. I was so engrossed in watching my majestic guests of honor that I almost forgot myself.

Suddenly Hazrat Abbas addressed to Haadi, "Have you taken his passport from my father?"

Haadi replied in the affirmative and repeated a verse from Surah-eRehman, "O groups of Jinns and humans, have you the strength to go out of the bounds of the heavens and the earth? Certainly not, without (God's gifted) strength."

On hearing this verse, Hazrat Abbas turned towards me and said, "Your remembering and recalling my father, the King of all saints, in your life, has proved to be your salvation. I welcome you with the news that you have been pardoned and absolved."

I bowed down and prostrated and kissed the floor, out of respect and gratefulness at being given this honor. I stood up but I was overcome with emotion at being treated so nicely and gently by these revered guests. Tears flowed down my cheek. Hazrat Habib Ibne Mazahir who was standing adjacent bent towards me and said softly, "Don't loose heart, you have been exempted from all hardships which would normally have confronted a traveller in this route. These two and their father will never forget you. Hazrat Ali helps his friends and believers in this world and it was he who sent his two sons to greet you, so that they may meet you and you may rest assured. And for your information, Hazrat Zainab has sent you her greetings. She says that she can never forget how you went barefoot on pilgrimage to her brother's shrine, shed tears for him and bore hardships including hunger and thirst and sickness on your trip."

I cannot possibly express how I felt on hearing this. All I could say was "May God's peace and blessing be on you and on them."

Then I asked Habib, "Why are these two dressed in full battle attire, when there is no war going on?"

Hazrat Habib's face became pale and he started crying. Then he replied, "In Karbala these two could not fight to their heart's content. They had intended to completely destroy the enemy and send them headlong to Hell, but God did not wish this and so their desire could not materialise. They bowed down to God's will, but their intention remained embossed in their hearts and here it has taken this form. They will remain attired in this way until our Twelfth Imam avenges the blood of Hussain (Peace be upon him)."

The guests then left and the room once again returned to its original size. Haadi and I were left alone. I remarked to Haadi, "I will never again visit my family because it only increases my sadness. The deeds, which on the face of it are being done for my spirit's benefit, were actually just for face-saving, for society's sake and to gain acclaim from the relatives. I have lost all hopes of receiving any benefit from them."

I will now rest contented with whatever I already have. As for any potential dangers, I can only hope that, Hazrat Abbas and Hazrat All Akbar will come to my rescue.'

Haadi replied "You don't require anything more. The first three steps should prove easy for you. This is because the first stage in the world is from birth to the age of three years when the child's brain is still devoid of sensibility. The next stage is up to fifteen years of age, when God does not yet hold him responsible for his deeds. The third stage is up to the age of eighteen years. In these three years though he becomes accountable, his mind is still immature. Man's deeds are judged keeping in view his intelligence.

"When Allah created intelligence He said, "I will base punishment and reward on you." The first three stages here correspond to those three stages, so they should prove easy for you, if any problem or danger does befall you, it will soon clear up by itself. So I don't consider it necessary to accompany you through these stages. I'll take your leave now. You'll find me waiting for you at stage four. Take your baggage and start tomorrow morning from here. Take that straight road going in the direction of Kaaba.

On hearing this I clung to Haadi and said "Haadi you know well I cannot bear to be separated from you. Even if the road is straight and wide and spacious, and the journey trouble-free but still, I would be alone, without you and a stranger in an unknown place. This I cannot bear. Even our Prophet (S.A.) has said to search a companion if one wishes to travel".

Haadi replied "You have to face these three stages alone, because in the world also I was not your companion during these three stages. I have been with you only since you became mentally mature. I belong to the exalted ones and our duty is to guide to well being and sublimity. Whatever befalls you in these stages will be due to your own actions. So blame yourself, not me".

Then he left, leaving me alone. I began to ponder over what he had said and finally reached the conclusion that he was right. I would indeed have to face it alone without my friend Haadi, the Abu Turab and Abu Wafa.

Allah has said, You will not find any change in the way and customs of Allah. The event of the world and the hereafter were interrelated and could not be separated. We have understood our earthly life. The hereafter follows a similar pattern and it is useless to dissent.

# 3
## Chapter

## JOURNEY TO THE FIRST STATION

I realized that it was time to leave. I picked up my Bag of Deeds and started on the road, which Haadi had pointed out. The road was clear, and a pleasant and cool breeze was blowing. I was fresh and eager to meet Haadi again at the fourth Station. I was walking briskly and I managed to cover quite some distance. Before noon, however, I was feeling a bit tired. It had become warmer, and I was thirsty. The pathway had narrowed and there were thorns here and there. Trying to keep free of these, I kept on until I reached the foot of a mountain and started climbing uphill.

The loneliness was getting on my nerves when suddenly I looked back and to my great relief, saw a person walking towards me on the same path. I was happy that I had at last found a companion to lessen the loneliness of the journey. When he came close, I saw that he was quite ugly to look at and had a distressed look. He had huge teeth, an over hanging upper lip and wide, fearful and stinking nostrils. He greeted me with "Saam Alaik" that is the 'l' in the salaam was missing. This was enough to put me on my guard, because this was not the Islamic way; in fact, was a sign of enmity. Furthermore it appeared to be intended that way, and did not seem to be a mistake, so I was on my guard and merely replied same to you."

Then I asked, "Where are you going?" He replied "Wherever you intend to go." I did not feel easy on having him as a companion. However I asked, "May I know who you are"? He replied "I am your alter ego. They call me Ignorance. My title is waywardness my family name Abu Lahaw (meaning father of playfulness i.e. to waste time in non-serious things). My aim is to create mischief, to ferment discord and dissension and to mislead people and cause them to go astray."

All this conversation further troubled and worried me. I thought that I
would have been better off alone, without such a person as companion.(10)

(10) (Traditions show that when Satan lost favor of Allah he was granted the wish that a child of his would be born whenever a human being was born, and he would remain the latter's constant companion even in Barzakh. His lob would be to mislead people. If the human being had overcome the Satanic commands and his own desires in the earthly life, then this twin would remain over powered in Barzakh and cause no harm. However, here he will cause problems and troubles to the extent that Man had sinned in his earthly life. As the Prophet had said "I too had this Satan but he embraced Islam on my hands."

The gist of this is that human being has his carnal and material desires from birth and no man is an exception. If he gives in to these and errs, he will subsequently regret, feel remorseful and consequently suffer. The successful one is he, who is so firm of mind that he always overpowers his desires. The ideal being was Holy Prophet (S.A.) who had completely vanquished and triumphed over desires.)

I asked him, "If we come to a diversion will you know

which route to take?"
He replied in the negative.

I then asked, "I am thirsty. Is there any water nearby?"

He replied "I don't know."

I asked, "Is our destination near?"

He again said, "I don't know."

I said, "Intelligence and wisdom go hand in hand with existence. How
is it that you do not know any thing?"

He said, "I only know that I have been at your side ever since you were
born. I have never separated from you except when Allah has especially favored you and you yourself have separated from me."

I soliloquized "Then this must be the Satan who used to mislead me in the world and on whose beckoning I used to sin. And even now he is not leaving me alone. This is indeed the height of enmity. Allah, Oh Allah, have mercy."
He kept following me, couple of paces behind. The road was uphill and steep and it was difficult going. At last I reached the top. I was tired, and so sat down to rest for awhile. Ignorance sat down beside me and said, "You seem to be tired. Do you want to know a short cut which will shorten your travel to only a fifth?"

I replied "In spite of your ignorance it seems you can pull miracles."

He said, "It's not that. Come here, I'll show you. See this

road on which you are travelling, though it's bright, is bent like a bow and is not less than 5 Km. The chord joining the two points of the arc is no more than one kilometer.

"Geometrically, an arc whether small or big is always bigger than its chord. So if we leave this popular road and instead take to the lesserknown path it'll be a short cut and no longer than 1 kilometer instead of five. Surely it's wiser to take the short cut."

I replied, "Don't be stupid. Don't you know that these highways are a result of the route being popular and constantly traversed. The people who chose it weren't senseless. And there's a famous saying that always travel on routes which are popular and favored by travelers."

He said, "You are indeed stupid. You are taking poets and storytellers to be wise men and you are content to follow in their foot steps. The path that I am pointing out is obviously shorter. And it is also possible that the people who chose the longer route had enough provision with them or had some means of conveyance. It is possible that they wanted to avoid that tunnel at the mouth of the chord, or maybe their mount could not pass through it. So tell me, why shouldn't the two of us take the short-cut?"

Here I committed the mistake of falling for what he said, mistaking him to be a well-wisher. We left the main road and took to the short cut. But it was not at all easy going here were deep ditches full of rubbish. The path was strewn with needle like thorns and we often came across snakes and scorpions. As soon as we would cross one ravine, we would reach another. It was so hot that my tongue was literally hanging out with thirst. My feet were also injured and bleeding. I was feeling afraid right down to the core of my heart.

My companion seemed to be enjoying my plight. He was joking and laughing at me. We traveled for what seemed to be ages and when at last we reached the highway again we had covered at least 10 Km. Each step had been an ordeal and I was dead tired. I had developed complete hatred for my twin and I told him so "I wish we had never met. I would be happier if we were as far apart as the two poles".

But he kept waiting for me whilst I sat down to rest. A bit rested I got up to resume my journey and he again started following me. Suddenly I spotted some greenery about one fourth kilometer away from the highway. Seeing his chance, ignorance again assaulted me. He came running to me and said, "Hey do you see the greenery over there? There's sure to be water there too. And you really are so thirsty. Let's go and have a look. Maybe we'll find a fresh water spring and you can get a cool drink. When we come back we'll resume our journey."

I can sincerely say that I did not want to obey him; but I was tired and thirsty and I knew that greenery was not possible without water![11]

((11) When man has to confront the consequences of his actions, he wishes he had never committed them. But this repentance is often not serious enough to stop him from again falling in for temptations and desires.)

So I again fell in his trap. We went towards it and the route proved to be an extremely difficult and painful one. When we reached, I saw that there was no sign of water anywhere. The ground was rocky and plain. There were huge black snakes visible everywhere. The greenery itself consisted of self-sustaining wild shrubs, which do not require additional water. Dejected, I turned back and after again crossing the trouble some path, reached the highway.

We were now in an open ground and all around us were fields full of watermelon plants, laden with fruits. Ignorance at once picked up one and busied himself eating it. He said 'Why don't you take one also. It'll kill your thirst'.

I said "It's somebody's personal property and it's not right to take without permission". Ignorance was so engrossed in eating that he was unmindful of the juice trickling down his beard and onto his chest. Shaking his head, he replied "Oh: Don't be so pious. Listen, firstly there's a good chance that the fields are self-growing and don't belong to anybody. Secondly, even if somebody owns them, Islamic Law allows travelers to consume the necessary minimum from the lands adjacent to the highways. And then, you look like you are about to die of thirst. In such conditions one is even allowed to consume dead bodies. In Surah-e-Baqra (Cow) Verse No. 173, God says:

"Whoever is driven to necessity, not desiring, nor exceeding the limit, then he is not guilty of sin, verily Allah is forgiving, merciful."

"And finally, you are no longer in Earth where you are required to live according to the Islamic laws. You are now in Barzakh and those laws are applicable there, not here. You religious people go to extremes. At times you give rulings which even God has not decreed."

Fool that I was, I again fell for him. I thought "Satan he maybe, but he certainly argues logically." I plucked a watermelon and tried to eat but it was so poisonously bitter, that it injured my mouth and throat. I threw it away and said, "These must be satanic watermelons, in fact of Ignorance."

He said, "No, no, you are mistaken. Its just a coincidence that particular melon was so bitter. Try another." So I tried a second and then a third but they were all the same. He was continuously eating and kept exclaiming, "Delicious melons, how extremely sweet." I snatched a slice from his hands and tasted it. It tasted similar to the ones I had eaten before, as bitter as one could imagine. I threw it away in disgust and exclaimed "God damn you, why are you eating these and claiming them to be tasty? I think snake venom must be less bitter." Now he said, "According to my taste, they are sweet and tasty melons. I am Ignorance and these melons are related to me. Whatever is good or beneficial for me is harmful for you, because I am Satan and you are a human. These are according to my taste and nature not to yours."[12]

((12) This is in accordance with the philosophical argument, the gist of which is that people judge things in accordance with their own nature. A sinner does not see wrong or bad in sins and disobedience in fact finds pleasure and contentment in these. Whereas a righteous person would be horrified at these and just the thought of committing evil would sicken him.)

Darky[13] quickly took the cue and was out onto the road in one bound. I too, tried to escape but could not manage it. The dog caught hold of my clothes and I fell down out of sheer fear at this sudden attack. The guard too reached the scene and joined in his stick. My pleas went unheard. I kept repeating that I had not eaten a single melon, but his answer was that as far as damage was concerned it was the same whether I had eaten them or thrown them away. At last, after he had given me a thorough beating, I managed to get away. I reached the road, but I was in a bad state, deeply injured and thirsty. I cried for Haadi, that he had left me alone to face such times.

((13) Henceforth the author has used the word "Darky" instead of Satan or Twin, in order to make obvious the darkness of Satanic incitements.)

Suddenly a vicious dog attacked us. Behind it was a guard armed with a stick. He was cursing us and it was clear that he too intended to attack.

Darky, however, was gleeful at his success. His laughter knew no limits. He watched me from afar and taunted me, "Go on, call Haadi. Do you really expect him to be helpful to you here, in this place? On the earth you had sown seeds for these sorrows in my garden; now is the time for tasting them. 'The World is the field where the Hereafter is cultivated and the Hereafter is the day of harvest.' You think yourself to be a scholar. Don't you know the Qur'an has said "Whoever has sinned as much as a grain, shall see it (in the hereafter)?" How can you expect Haadi to help you in spite of these laws of God? Admitted that we will soon reach those places where Haadi will be present but don't forget I too will be there. You will have to face calamities at places where Haadi will be useless for you. Did not Haadi himself tell you that whenever you sinned he went away, leaving you alone, though he returned to you when you repented? Don't you even remember your own Prophet's tradition, "A faithful does not commit adultery as long as he is a true faithful." Hence Haadi was never present with you at these occasions[14] when you sinned, so how can he help you now, when you have to pay for those deeds of yours." I thought that there was no solution for this accursed being. He was too well informed for my comfort. I stopped calling for Haadi, opened my bag and took out an apple. It was a juicy one and refreshed me and quenched my thirst. Even my bruises became well. I got up and resumed my journey.

((14) From the traditions of the Infallible we gather that faith is not a permanent resident of the faithful's heart. If he sins, faith leaves him to return only when he repents. As faith is divine and godly gilt it does not remain with the faithful if he indulges in sins. (e.g. lying, adultery, fraud, rivalry, etc.) and as faith departs he is engulfed in Darkness and Ignorance.
May God grant us all the desire and chance to repent truly.) After sometime I reached bisection with one road leading to an open, airy and bright city and the other towards a desolate place. A Sentry was standing guard at the bisection. I approached him and said,

"Comrade, if possible can you prevent Darky from following me? He has already caused me a great deal of trouble today."

The guard replied, "Just as the human's shadow is inseparable from the body, so is Darky. Tonight, however, he will not be able to approach you, because they are not allowed inside the City of Light. They will stay the night in that desolate and dark place on your left. When you resume your journey he will again be at your side. However, it is possible that he will not trouble you so much then".

I entered the bright and developed city. This was the first station. There were beautiful buildings; flowing lakes, greenery, and trees laden with fruits; beautiful servants with eloquent speech; delicate and tasty food, and delicious drinks.

I felt so happy and contented, especially as this came after the horrible and burdensome journey and the troubles that I had borne because of my Darky. These were now compensated by the Edenic place, and had it not been for the urge to meet Haadi at the fourth station, I would have been contented to stay here only.

Here I also met a few of my students who had died a few years before me. We spent the night here. In the morning, the breeze was scented with the smell of fresh fruits. We strolled in the city, chatting and inquiring about each other's welfare because in the hereafter one can only inquire about another's welfare at such stops as one is too busy to even think of another when he is travelling. As the Qur'an says, on the Day of Judgment each man will be engrossed in his own self, oblivious of others". We were also thankful to be rid of the Darkies.

In short, we were completely happy here, with the best of people, service and food. The best thing was that the ugly Darkies were not near us. We were thankful to God, that for our small deeds on the earth he had so richly rewarded us. As Qur'an says in Surah-e-Safat verse 61, "For the like of this all strivers should strive.

# 4
Chapter

## JOURNEY TOWARDS SECOND STATION

The bell peeled 'Come towards the best deed'. This was a sign that, it was time to depart for the next station. We picked up our respective packs and luggage and started. We reached bisection and to our great dismay saw the Darkies, who were approaching us like black smoke.

I asked a Duty Officer present if there was any way to avoid their company. He replied "These are only the faces of your own base and beastly selves (traits) like injustice, pride, desire, anger etc. Hence, if you had not separated from them in you earthly life, how can you separate them from yourselves now. But they are of different kinds and all are not bad. Some are purely black, some are mixed black and white and some white and bright. And they are named accordingly e.g. "Ammara" (inciter to evil), "Lawwama (Helper towards repentance), Mutmainna (contented with God). If any of you have the white Mutmainna for your companion, then he is a companion worth having. He is a useful, beneficial, and sometimes better and more sublime then even angel. Mutmainna (Contentment) was in fact God's gift to you but you wasted it by your ungratefulness and carnal desires. You will now reap whatever you have sown in your earthly material life. Then you were free to sow whatever you wished, but now you have no choice but to reap accordingly, whether good or bad. As God has said, Do you (cause the seeds to) grow or are we the growers?"

No sooner was this said, then the Darkies reached us and each of us had his particular companion alongside as we went forward. But our group had somewhat separated, some were left behind with their Darkies and some were travelling besides me. I myself had my Darky by my side until we reached a mountain. The path here was very narrow and difficult. On one side of the mountain was a deep moat, but it was difficult terrain to cross. An idea occurred to me that I should go to the summit because extremely warm air from the moat was suffocating me. Suddenly my satanic twin come near and said, You are correct in thinking of going to the top. Not only is the air from the moat so extremely warm and humid, there are also poisonous animals there. And also from the top you'll be able to look down around you on all sides."

On the earth I had been in the habit of speaking loudly in order to impose my authority on others and also I always had the ambition to reach higher and sublime levels, so I liked the idea and decided to reach the top. But there was no direct path to the summit, so I walked along the mountain wall and even then it was difficult going. A couple of times I slipped. Once I stumbled and almost fell down in the moat but just saved myself by catching hold of a thorny bush, badly injuring my hands and feet in the process. Further down the road, I again fell: my nose hit the ground, broke and started bleeding profusely,[15] I remarked, 'It is very troublesome to reach the top. It might have been better to have traveled through the moat."

(15) (The author has hinted that whoever is proud and arrogant in the world, God will punish him in the Hereafter

in such a way as break his pride and turn it to dust.)

The accursed being laughed and said, "He who is proud in the world, God will break his back, and he who tries to be higher than others, God will rub his nose in dust (that is, lower him)." I really wonder at you, that you have read all this, but have never acted accordingly. "Taste it, you were (thought yourself to be) Respected and Elite" (Surah-e-Dukhan verse 25).[16]

(16) (Abu Jahl used to say, "I am the Respected and Elite. On the day of Judgement, he and others like him will be addressed 'O Respected and Elite, taste the punishment".)

I kept walking as he talked, bearing the hardships, one after another. At last I came out of the plateau, through which there had been no visible path. Though with injured body and feelings.

Now when I turned back, I saw that my companions, who had been just behind me, were stumbling and falling down into the deep and dark moat. They were crying in pain and anguish and their Darkies were laughing wickedly and gleefully.
Finally, we reached a road where the going was much easier. There were no new problems here except that I was extremely thirsty. My Darky again tried a couple of time to trap me by his deceiving and captivating arguments but I did not pay heed. At times, I must admit, I felt like giving in but still I resisted. When he realized that I just would not give in, he himself fell back.[17]

(17) (If one practices denying his self and desires, after a while desires and whims will no longer trouble him.) But alertness and vigilance will have to be a constant practice.)

After quite some time, I reached a garden. The path itself passed through its center. I spotted a pond, with people sitting around it, eating from trays full of fruits. As soon as they saw me, they stood up respectfully greeted me and asked me to join them. I asked, "Who are you and why are these fruits here?"

They replied, "Each of us had been fasting when we died. This is the Iftari sent by the Benevolent, Merciful Allah for our supper. We believe that you too can partake of it. Admitted that you were not fasting at the time of your death but you have often played host to people who were fasting and arranged their iftari so you have a right to these fruits." I sat down with them and ate a little. It quenched my thirst and healed my heart and body. They inquired about my travel and I replied "Thank God it's past. And my sorrows and troubles have disappeared now that I have met you. But I had to leave my friends and companions behind as their Darkies entrapped them. My Darky too tried his level best but I did not fall for him. Now he has himself fallen back. I hope he never catches up with me again". They laughed and replied "Its not so. In this garden they can only use their weapons of deception and lying but when we will proceed from here they are sure to reach us through a short cut and will literally tight to destroy us.

I asked, "We don't have any weapons how will we win?" They replied, "If in the world you denied yourself and went against your desires, and so prepared your defense, then these defensive weapons will, God willing, have reached the battle field in advance. As Qur'an says in Surah-eAnfal, verse 60, "Make preparation for them (the enemy) from whatever possible, strength, well-bred horses (cavalry) in order to frighten your enemies and the enemies of God."

I said, "I always thought that this verse referred to making preparations for Holy War." They replied, the laws of Qur'an are universally applicable and not restricted to the earth. Otherwise the Qur'an, would be faulty and lacking. But it is not so because it is a divine gift and has been revealed unto the last of the Prophets."

# 5 Chapter

## JOURNEY TO THE THIRD STATION

We got up and resumed our journey. The road was good and it was easy going. On both sides were dense trees laden with fruits and a lake of cool and sweet water flowed alongside the path. A pleasant breeze further refreshed the mind. It was as if we were beholding the very image of the Beauty of God.

The journey passed without any problems worth mentioning. It had been so easy that we were not in the least tired or travel-weary when we reached the third station. Each of us was given a separate palace for our stay. The bricks of these palaces were of silver and gold. The palaces were elaborately equipped and furnished and not a single thing was lacking. The delicate crockery, exquisite flooring and murals were unbelievable. The servants were beautiful, well mannered, eloquent and well dressed. They were busy, moving all around us. Making arrangements for our comfort, as if they were the very pictures described in Qur'an "Around them circle beautiful, ever living boys (servants). And "when you see them, you will imagine them to be spread pearls and when you behold, then you will behold bounties and a large power."

I felt shy asking such people for service. Suddenly, I spotted a large mirror and in it I saw the sublime station to which by his grace the Exalted Allah had elevated me. I felt high on being so honored and rested back comfortably.

Night fell and the palace became illuminated. Careful scrutiny revealed that the light was emerging from the branches of the trees. This light was so bright that a thousand of our electric bulbs would not be able to match it. The palace and the gardens were bright with this light. I was wondering at this spectacle when a voice called out verse 35 of Surah-e-Noor "Allah is the light of the Heavens and the Earth. The similitude of this light is as a niche wherein is a lamp. The lamp is in a glass. The glass is as if it were a shining star, lit from a blessed tree, the olive, neither of the East nor of the West, whose oil glows forth (of itself) though fire did not touch it; light upon light; Allah guides unto his light, whomsoever he wills."

I at once realized that the light was of the tree of Muhammad (S.A.) and his progeny and this city, the city of love. Only those people were allowed to stay here who had the ultimate love for Muhammad (S.A.) and his progeny. Here the residents were busy, recalling the sublime qualities of Muhammad (S.A.) and his progeny and asking God to send his peace and blessings upon them as through them only the human race had acquired knowledge of Allah and the correct ways to worship him.

Here we were in great comfort. Out hearts were full of thankfulness to God for his grace and bounty, and to Muhammad (S.A.) and his progeny for having guided us towards the correct path. On the gate was a sign saying in bold letters "The love of Ali is such a quality that in its presence no sin can harm."[18]

(18) (This tradition is believed universally by all Muslims. It means that, anyone who truly loves Ali, does not sin because naturally he tries to follow his ideal through thoughts and deed. Hence Ali's love acts as a shield against committing sins.

If one finds him to be proclaiming love for Ali but also committing sins, he should closely observe and question this love. As to whether there really is true love in his heart and if so, is it just for the name "ALI" or whether it is for Ali's qualities, habits, life style, ideals, thoughts and deeds? Are all these acceptable to him and do these appeal to him, because "ALI" represents these and not merely a historical name.)

# 6
Chapter

## THE FOURTH STATION AND REUNION WITH HAADI

In the morning we started for the next station. The road was clear and easy. On both sides there were lush green trees in full blossom. Cool water flowing softly in the lakes, and a pleasant breeze, all these made it a perfect scene, beyond description. We reached the outskirts and it seemed as if its beauties accompanied us for a little while outside the city in order to see us out.

The path was now no longer clear and clean; in fact, it had become narrow and rocky. Then it passed through a twisting and snaking valley. Had we not been so many people in our group, we would surely have lost our way. We reached a spot where numerous forks led toward the left and it was not easy to decide which one to chose. As we went on, we suddenly saw the Darkies approaching us from one of the paths on the left.

The moment I saw my Darky, I felt overcome with mixed emotions of grief, sorrow and anger. In the brief moment that my eyes were on him, my foot struck a stone and was badly injured. I limped on but could only manage a slow pace and was soon left behind as my other companions went forward with quick steps. Darky stayed on my left until we reached bisection. I could not choose which fork to take. Seeing my momentary hesitation, Darky approached and said, 'What are you thinking?" Then pointing towards the left fork, he said, "This path is the correct one." So saying, he took a few steps towards the left, expecting me to follow. However, instead of following him, I choose to go the other way, in the opposite direction.[19]

(19) (It is an accepted fact that the way to happiness and success lies in opposing the satanic incitements and desires.)

Darky kept insisting that I follow him but I did not pay him the least heeds, because I had already suffered enough and each time he had been the cause. I thought of Hazart Ali's words "To try him whom you have already tried (and he has failed) is stupidity".

In a short while we were out of the valley. The road again became clear and the visibility also increased. Further on the dark shapes of trees in a meadow could be seen. I at once understood that this was the Fourth Station where Haadi had promised to meet me. The thought of seeing Haadi again, spurred me on to the extent that I almost started running and left a dejected Darky well behind.[20]

(20) (As said before, if satanic incitements and desires are constantly opposed, they gradually lose the power to misguide and doing good continuously further increases one's eagerness and appetite for good deeds.)
Soon I saw Haadi waiting for me at the city gate. When I saw him thus waiting as he had promised he would, I ran to him, and greeted and embraced him. I felt as if I had been granted a fresh life. Hand in hand we entered the city. Haadi guided me to a palace, which had been especially

built for me. It was most comfortable and peaceful here. I rested a while then had some refreshments.

Seeing me fresh once more, Haadi asked,

"Well, how is it with you? Tell me how was your journey through the last three stages?" I answered "All praise is for God, the Creator and sustainer of all Universe. He showers us with bounties in spite of our sins. Whatever it was that befell me was naught but punishment for my own deeds for which I alone was responsible. And if you had been with me, Darky would never have dared to mislead me. Anyhow, all that is now past. What matters is, I have finally reached here and met you again. The ordeal is over and the sorrows forgotten".[21]

(21) (Possibly (a) knowledge and (b) piety as they have served the purpose of a guiding stick and a shield in the world and so might take these farms in the hereafter.)

Haadi said, "Well I wasn't with you so you kept falling in Darky's traps; but even now when I am with you, do not imagine yourself to be completely safe from him. My position is merely that of God's decisive arguments; my job is merely to warn and alert you against Darky's deceptions. But never forget that Darky is equipped with powerful tools. He will try his best to mislead you. And this time if you fall in his trap and are misled away from the straight path it could spell your end, and I would be unable to help you as I have delivered to you the ultimate proof. In these stations you have only a stick and a shield for your protection. But even these will prove insufficient. So, as today is Friday, go visit your family and see if they have done any good deed on your behalf which can help you) here."[22]

(22) (Spirits are sometimes able to visit their families, according to certain traditions).

I said, "Haadi, you know well that I have given up all hopes from that quarters. Their only interest lies in their own selves. The living forget the dead very easily. When I visited them last time, I had not been dead even a week, but in spite of it, whatever they were doing was only for their own sake."

Haadi said, "No, you must go there today. I'm sure they must have remembered the Holy Prophet's tradition that 'Remember your dead with good (deeds or words'). 'And if you go there they might recall you, since it might cause Allah to remind them of you.[23] And even if you have lost hopes of their helping you, at least have hopes from Allah. If one keeps knocking, the door is bound to yield. And never lose hope in Allah. 'Allah's mercy is close to the Good-doers'.

On Haadi's insistence, I went to my old home. I saw that the name, respect and position it had held in the past were no more. The gate was closed to the public unlike the way it had been in the past. My family's earning and livelihood had dwindled almost to nil. My children lay listless and none came to inquire their welfare. It saddened me beyond words. Compulsively, I turned towards Allah: 'O Most Merciful, have pity on my children and myself, because you are the lord of all'. It seemed as if my praying for them refreshed my remembrance in their hearts because they started recalling me and the good time they had in my lifetime. They wept and prayed for me.

(23) (When a person's mind attentively concentrates on another, it is possible that it causes the other to

compulsively think of him.)

When I returned, I found a beautiful and healthy horse standing besides Haadi. I asked Haadi where it had come from, and he replied smilingly, "your family prayed for you and God's blessing has come to you in this form.[24]

"And it is just as well because it would have been very difficult to continue our journey on foot. Also your prayer for your family has been granted and henceforth they will live in comfort and well being.

"You can see yourself how beneficial your visit has proved for all of you. It seems that on earth people are careless about praying for each other, as they are ignorant of its benefits. The Holy Prophet has said 'If three days pass without people inquiring the well-being of each other then the bond of faith between them breaks."

I returned to my room and was pleasantly surprised to find a beautiful and lovely maiden sitting on the couch. Her eyes were bright and her shining face seemed to illuminate the whole room. Haadi announced, 'This maiden has been wed to you and especially sent here for tonight from the Valley of Peace'. So saying, he left.

The two of us were left alone. When I approached her, she stood up to greet me, and respectfully kissed my hands. We then sat down next to each other. We spent the night in blissful comfort.

(24) (Praying sincerely for the dead can improve their lot as God may bless them through his mercy and forgiveness.)

# 7 Chapter

## TRAVEL TO THE NEXT STATION WITH HAADI

When morning came, Haadi arrived. We were to depart for the next station. I got up, dressed and mounted my horse. My walking stick was in my hand and my sword by my side. Haadi gave me my Visa, which he said would be required. We started and were soon out of the city limits. Here the ground was sandy and slippery like encountered in jungles. I also saw some odd creatures like monkeys. Then I realized that they were humans, as they had no tails, walked on two legs, and had no body hair, only their faces were of monkeys. Blood and puss emitted from their private parts accompanied by an unbelievable stink.

I asked Haadi, "Who are these creatures, and what land is this? The stink is so bad, I feel as if my head will burst."

He replied, "This is the Land of Lust and Desire. These people were adulterers. Beware you don't deviate from the straight path or it might well spell the end for you."

Fearful of going astray, I tightened the rein. Though the path was straight it was marshy and slippery quagmire. At times my mount would sink down to his knees in the marshy earth.[25]

(25) (There is a hint here of how carefully one should live in the world. Keeping tight rein on his desires, especially for women, because such pleasure is nowadays easily available. And if one is not extremely vigilant to restrict his desires to his wife, he is sure to indulge, to whatever little extent, in unlawful and forbidden pleasures for which he will have to suffer. And God forbid if, he should commit the extreme act, then for such people there is harsh punishment unless they sincerely repent and are forgiven by God.)

I thought, "It is indeed a blessing that I have this mount. May God have mercy on my family that they provided this for me. It is indeed true that, "He who marries safeguards half his religion, and he should be watchful of Allah in the other half.[26]

(26) (Being married and having lawful means for fulfilling one's natural and instinctive sexual desires helps man to a great extent to reject extramarital temptations.)

Now we saw some people resembling animals. They were hanging from nails on posts and their testicles had been nailed to the posts with iron pins. Some were also being whipped with iron rods and they were screaming in pain like yelping dogs. But the men with the whips in their hands would reply:

"Go away and keep quiet".[27] It was as if the scene in Surah-e-Sajda verse 12 is in front of us:

"If you see when the sinners stand in front of God. With their heads bent low: God, we have seen and heard. Now send us back that we may do good deeds. We have now attained certainty". These were people who used to indulge in various forbidden sexual pleasures.

(27) (The Arabic word is used to order away dogs.)

Suddenly the Darkies arrived. They literally attacked some people. And tried to frighten the horses. They also beckoned to us to try the land adjoining the path. I saw that the adjoining land was so hard that the horses feet did not even leave an impression on the ground. But I obeyed Haadi's orders. I did not care whether the going was tough or easy, my only aim was to follow the straight path and not to deviate from it. (Because, salvation lies only in following the straight path.)

I saw that those who had obeyed their Darkies beckoning were able to manage only a few steps before sliding dawn up to their necks in the marsh. It did not seem possible that they would ever manage to come out Some did manage it, but they were so filthy black and covered from top to toe with the mire, that they could not be recognized. In a short time, the mire seemed to melt away the flesh from their bodies as if it was not mire at all but hot charcoal.

This scene scared and subdued me firmly and carefully, I held the rein and thought.

"Praise is for God who prevented me from committing sins."

(28) (Those who deviated from the path were those who had deviated on earth.)

(29) (Sins committed leave their impression on the mind, heart and spirit and spoil one's self and character.)

I could hear other travelers too loudly thanking God, and expressing their gratefulness. I remarked to Haadi:

"Our Holy Prophet had said that if you see anybody in difficulties, softly thank God that you are not suffering similarly. But do not thank God loudly, that the other person might overhear and be hurt."

Haadi replied, "That was for your earthly life because there, all believers of God are to be respected. But here is the stage of reward and punishment. So thank God loudly in order that those who are being punished may hear and suffer more and also, so that whatever was hidden to them may come out in the open, darkness may be replaced with light, blindness with sight and slumber with awakening. And they may realize that the earthly life as they led it was in reality a Dead City of Darkness and as verse 64 of Surah-e-Ankabut says, "The abode of the hereafter is, in fact, true life."

On hearing this I thanked God in louder tones. Then I saw that the problems seemed to increase for the wretched people, around me. The earth quaked, the wind raged, and the sky darkened. Hails resembling stones were falling. All around us was a dreadful scene and the wretched persons seemed to sink further down in the mire. Whenever they would manage to come out a heavy stone would fall from the sky burying them down again. Trembling with fear at this state of affairs I asked Haadi, "Which land is this and who are these people who are being punished so severely?"

Haadi who was flying above my head had himself gone pale and weak with fear. He replied, "This is also a Land of Lust. These people were homosexuals. Now increase your speed, so that we may get out of here as soon as possible. If we stay here longer I am afraid we too might get caught in this punishment. "He who is complacent or unobjecting at the deeds of a people and who does not leave them (at once) after being with them, will be included with, and treated as, one of them."(30)

(30) (in this world too, one has to struggle and strive continuously against sins and desires and try continuously to improve oneself or else he falls stagnant and his qualities might rest and even recede. Leaving sins and bad habits, increasing religious knowledge and improving on one's deeds is a never-ending struggle.)

I asked, "Is the slime and mire in fact, the substance of lust which has taken this form here? My mount cannot even go forward."

He said, "Yes, that is so. But there is no other way out. You will just have to strive more. Cover your head with this shield so that the stones do not hit you and whip your mount forward, so that with God's blessing you may get out of here. As verse 98 of Surah-e-Nisa says, "Was not the earth of God spacious, that (in order to be able to obey God) you could migrate?"

We traveled only a couple of miles more to find ourselves out of the bedeviled place. I thanked God, and gathered myself once more. I whipped the horse a few times and suddenly he was off like a shot.(31)

(31) (If one decides firmly to leave his wrong ways and takes the right initiative, the rest becomes easy. God has promised that if one goes towards him a little bit, God will respond by coming forward a great deal more.)
Haadi who all this time had been travelling right above me

like a falcon was left far behind.(32)

(32) (If man conquers his desires then in God's eyes he has a higher rank than even angels.)

"Vie in hastening towards your lord's forgiveness and a garden whose width is as that of the heavens and the earth." (Surah-e-Hadeed verse 21)
Suddenly the accursed Darky arrived. My mount shied and reared at his sight throwing me down.(33)

(33) (One gets carried away by success, (even if it is spiritual) and becomes heedless of the scheming of Satan.)

I was hurt badly and the horse's forelegs got trapped in the mire and freeing him again was quite a problem. After great difficulty I succeeded. Haadi arrived just then, and rubbed me gently with his hands healing my bruises. Then he helped me to mount again and secured me safely in the saddle and taking hold of the reins led the way until we were at last out of the place.
I complained to Haadi, "As soon as you leave, Darky arrives and always causes trouble."

Haadi replied, "No, it is the other way round. As soon as he arrives, I leave. And this too, is because of your own deeds."

In front was yet another Land of Desire, which we entered. Here there were people who used to be very heavy eaters. On the right were those who only ate from rightful and lawful means but always used to overeat and stuff themselves full. Their faces were now like donkeys, and cows, and they were being punished but lightly. On the left however, were those who had been mindless about right and wrong, lawful and forbidden, about wealth which was their own and that which had been forcibly or fraudulently taken from others. They had greedily laid their hands on all within reach. Now they had huge bellies and lean limbs and their faces resembled those of pigs and bears and they were being severely punished. It was as if their bellies were full of fire. "These peoples are like cattle, in fact more astray." (Surah-e-Araaf, verse 179)

We quickly walked past this place, and reached another. Here was a rest house in a barren and deserted field in which nothing grew. A few travelers of the Hereafter were resting here, and eating from their backpacks. As my limbs were still very painful due to my fall, Haadi took out an ointment from my pack and massaged me with it. Instantly the pain vanished and the bruises healed. I asked "Haadi, what medicine is that?"

He said, "This was the hidden praise on earth. Whenever you were blessed with any gift, you used to thank Allah and praise him in your heart. Just as on earth praising Allah is a remedy for everything except death, so in the Hereafter it is a remedy for all difficulties and problems for him who used to praise Allah on earth. In the tradition of Qudsi Allah says, "My servant praised and thanked me, believing that all the bounties he received were from me and also believed that the dispersing and easing of all his problems had been through my blessing. So, O Angels, bear witness that I will increase my blessings and bounties on him on earth and in the Hereafter, and as I solved his problems on the earth so will I help him in the Hereafter."

# 8
Chapter

## THE STATION OF BLISS AND PEACE

We spent the night here, and resumed our journey in the morning. Haadi had already informed me that by evening we would be out of the land of Desire but then we would have to face the punishments due to the sins of the Tongue. The previous punishments were due to indulgence in immoral sexual pleasures and these would be due to the sins of the tongue, but these would be as harsh as those. He had said that there would be no provision of water or food and so it would be advisable to carry some water on the horse and I should myself travel on foot. He also told me to carry my shield as it would prove very useful.

I asked, "What is this shield made of?"

He replied, "This is the result of your fasts. You fasted and remained hungry and thirsty to please God and these fasts prevented you not only from immoral sexual indulgence, but also in fact from disobedience of all kinds. "Fasting is a shield to protect from the Fire of Hell."

We had only just started when Darky appeared. I said, "Be gone, O cursed being?" He said, "Why don't you yourself move away from me, instead?"

So, I moved a few steps away and continued my journey with Haadi, but Darky remained alongside on the left.

On both sides various animals were visible, e.g. dogs, wolves, monkeys, rats, snakes, scorpions, sheep etc., all of different colors. They were fighting amongst themselves, attacking, and tearing away at each other, whenever they got the chance. Flames emerged from the ears and mouths of some of them. Sometimes they would see a mirage and would go there in hopes of finding water, but finding it dry would return dejected. Some were eating the dead carcasses of others. Some would fall in dark and deep wells and as they would fall, huge flames would emerge.

I asked Haadi, "Who are these wells for?"

"They are meant for people who laugh at other faithfuls and make fun of them, whether through words hints, gestures, making faces, eye-movements etc. This is their destination. As God has said, "Hell is for the faultfinders and insulters." As for those who are eating carcasses, they were the backbiters. And the ones with flaming ears, they used to listen to others backbiting. And these dogs, wolves and cats fighting each other used to curse, blame and insult each other. And those with yellow faces and two tongues were the faultfinder, liars and complainers.

Here the air was extremely hot. I kept asking Haadi for water Sometimes he would give me a little, and sometimes none. He kept saying that the journey was lengthy and our store of water meager, which we would have to make last until the end.[34]

(34) (Hazrat Ali: "How lengthy is the journey (of the

Hereafter) and how meager our store of provisions (that is, good deeds which would help there.)

I asked him why he had taken so little to start with, and he replied, "You did not make yourself capable of taking more."

I asked, "Why did the capability decrease?"

He said, "You are yourself to blame, because you did not drink much of piety then, and so your capacity cannot increase now. The more watchful and pious you had been on earth, the more water you would have had now. Nothing can be done about it now. Haven't you read the opening verse of 'Surah-e-Mominoon', "Certainly the faithful have succeeded, who used to be fearful in their prayers and abstained from meaningless pastimes? You neither abstained from such pastimes nor were you fearful in your prayers. Obviously you will now reap what you had sown.

"Whoever has done a grain of good shall see it and, whoever has done a grain of evil shall see it."

Then he pointed in a certain direction and asked me what I could see there. It seemed like white and black and flames all mixed together.

But when I looked carefully it was a green garden, with dense trees, full of fruits. Suddenly I realized that they were burning. Shocked, I turned to Haadi and asked, "What is happening there?" He replied that the garden had been made from the praise and remembrance of God by the faithfuls, but when these faithfuls lied or indulged in backbiting, or insulting, the garden went up in flames. That is, their sins caused the reward of their good deeds to go waste. Had their faith been strong enough, they would have given more thought and importance to the gardens they had prepared and would not have allowed them to burn by indulging in such acts.[35]

(35) (The Holy Prophet once told his companions that whoever says "La ilaha illal'lah" (there is no power but God) once, the angels prepare a tree for him in Heaven. They remarked, 'In that case, by now we must be having a garden each'. He replied, 'Yes, but on the condition that you abstain from sins, like conceit because it destroys the trees.)

When their owners reach here and realize what has happened, they will be extremely sorry, but sorrow, would now be useless. That is why all the Prophets had continuously warned about the effects of good and bad deeds, as these cannot be seen whilst on earth. In the beginning of the Qur'an, God linked piety to faith in the unseen: "This is guidance for the pious, those who have faith in the unseen and who stand firm their prayers."

When we reached near these burnt gardens suddenly I felt a cool breeze which blew away the ashes. In a little while the garden was once more green, with lush trees laden with fruits, chirping birds and cool lakes. On earth, the faithful must have either repented for past sins or had sent fresh deeds. I thought that if the earthlings were aware of what I had just seen, they would die with sorrow at having ever allowed their gardens to burn. Haadi informed me that this was the first land of the Valley of Peace and here there was peace on all sides. He said, "Rest your stick and your shield on the saddle and let the mount graze in the field so that he too may be rested by the time we are ready, leave.

Haadi then said that we could take a break from our journey. And stay in that place for ten days, in order that, I might recover after the tiring travel. And regain strength, which would be required in the forthcoming leg, as there we would have to face many thieves, highwaymen and pirates. And as I did not have the required strength to face them he suggested that I should visit my old home once more, the coming Friday, to check if my family had sent me any gifts which could prove useful.

I said, "Haadi, you yourself told me that we had arrived in the Valley of Peace. Now you expect me to believe that there are robbers and pirates in this valley? I feel that you are merely trying to dissuade me. I certainly did not expect this from you." So saying, I started crying.

Haadi said, "My friend, do not distrust me. You are not aware how dark and narrow the coming route is. Our route in the Valley of Peace lies adjacent to the Valley of Punishment where all sorts of punishments are being meted out. The slightest slip will mean a fall into that valley where even I would be unable to help you. And you are aware that Darky is constantly trying to mislead you. If you don't spend the next ten days here to recover, you might well have to spend two months in the Valley of Punishment."

I said, "Do you mean to say that I have to face the stage of the Bridge (Pul-e-Sirat) now?! This I cannot believe."

He said, "I have already told you that whatever is happening here is the similitude of the events to take place on the Day of Judgment. Consider this route to be the image of that Bridge. These stages have to be crossed and it will be wise to provide for them in good time.

Anyhow, Friday night I went home once again. There I saw that my wife had married again and was busy trying to make her new husband happy. My children had separated and gone their different ways and were running individual and separate businesses. Dejected and forlorn I sat on a branch near my house. I could see that people were deeply engrossed in their worldly affairs. I thought, if only they would think of their own hereafter even if for a moment. But no, they were busy planning their future, and their children's future. I recalled the Holy prophet's tradition: "In the last ages, wives will prove to be the undoing of men; and when not wives, then children and relatives".

I was deep in such thoughts when suddenly my eyes fell on a room in my house. My sons and their wives had gathered and were sitting with their children talking with each other and eating some fruits. One of them said to the other, "The tree which bore this fruit had been sown by our late father. Now he is lying in a grave under mounds of Earth and we are eating its fruit."

The other son replied, "How wrong you are! He must be eating tastier fruits in Heaven."

The first one said, "Yes, you are right. He used to love me a lot. To please me and make me happy, he often used to buy me gifts. May God bless him."
May God bless him. He used to buy gifts for me too. He would buy books and pens whenever I required. To be sure, he was a religious man and it was his wish that we too would become Religious" said the other.

They spoke well of me for sometime, then one remarked that as it was Thursday night, it would be good to recite Quran for me. One of them started reciting Soora Dukhan and the other Surah Dahr for me. I cannot describe how happy this made me. I prayed for their well being and returned to my current abode

# 9
Chapter

## THE LAST STATION: THE VALLEY OF PEACE

When I returned I saw that my mount was ready for the journey and Haadi was packing a portmanteau on it. I asked him where it had come from. He said that an angel had just delivered it saying that it contained a gift from Hazrat Fatema Zehra (A.S.). This was the result of Surah Dukhan as this Surah was related to her and the other contained a gift from Hazrat Ali as Surah-e-Dahr was connected to him. They had sent these gifts and had requested that we take a path well away from Valley of Barhoot (Valley of Punishment) so that the hot air from it would not bother me.

I asked, "Is it possible to open them and see the contents?"

He said, "Not now, they are not required yet. When it becomes necessary, they will open by themselves.'

I was dazed with happiness. I climbed my mount and started".

After some time, we reached the Land of Greed and Avarice. There we saw people with faces like dogs, some of them were healthy and strong, others weak and frail.

There were dead bodies lying here and there.(36) The dogs would approach these in order to eat them, but would fall to fighting amongst themselves. They would fight each other fiercely until they were almost dead with the fatigue and tension; and the carcasses remained untouched. Fresh packs would then approach. The stronger ones would attack the weaker once and make them run away but were also unable to enjoy the carcasses because of their own internal competition for supremacy and each one's desire to have all of it alone, without sharing. The whole ground seemed to be one big battlefield. The world is a dead body and those who desire it, dogs.'

(36) The real value of worldly goods in the eyes at God and the Infallibles, In Nahjul Balagha, Hazrat Ali (A.S.) calls the world and its possessions "dead bodies."

Some dogs were eating these carcasses but smoke was bellowing from their heads and fire from their behinds and even other dogs would not approach them. Haadi informed me that they used to take bribes and used to embezzle or steal wealth belonging to orphans.

"Those who eat the wealth of orphans eat fire in their stomachs."(37)

(37) There is a famous tradition of the Holy Prophet (Peace be upon him) which describes almost similar conditions. This is quoted in the book 'Roahe Rehan' from the book 'Kaafi' quoting Hazrat Ali (A.S.) as saying that he and Hazrat Fatima (A.S.) once visited the Holy Prophet (Peace be upon him) and found him in tears. They asked him the cause and he replied, "O Ali the night that I went for Meraj (Ascension) I saw some women of my Ummah who were being so severely punished that I became

concerned for them and started crying. I saw a woman who had been hung by her breasts. Then I saw a second woman who was eating her own flesh and a fire raged below her. A third woman was hanging by her tongue and boiling water was being poured down her throat. A fourth was bent double, hand and feet tied together, snakes and scorpions crawling all over her. A fifth was deaf, dumb and blind, enclosed in a cage of fire, her brains oozing out of holes in her skull. Her body was breaking to pieces due to leprosy.

Another was hung by her feet, inside and over. Yet another woman's body was being shredded to pieces by scissors made of fire. One woman had a head of a pig and a body of a donkey and was being given several kinds of punishments. Another had the face of a dog, fire was entering her body from her behinds and coming out of her mouth and the angels were giving her a beating with iron rods."

Hazrat Fatima (A.S.) then inquired of her father (Peace be upon him) "Pray, tell me, what had these women done?" He (Peace be upon him) replied, "Listen, beloved one, she who was hanging by her breasts used to deny her husband his rightful pleasure. The one hanging by her feet used to go out of her house without her husband's permission. The one eating her own flesh used to beautify her and show her body to men other then her husband. The one who was tied hands and feet together, with snakes and scorpions on her, never used to care about the filthy and unclean, or 'Najaasat and was not careful about bathing regularly after menses, intercourse etc, thus taking her prayers lightly. The deaf, dumb and blind used to bear children through adultery but would claim they were her husband's. The one whose body was being cut by scissors made of fire never took care of her Hijab in front of Na-Mahrams (men other than those allowed to see her). The one whose body was being burned and who was eating her own intestines used to provide other women to men for sex. The one with the face of a pig and body of a donkey was backbiter and a liar. And the one with the face of a dog, with fire entering from her behinds and coming out of her face, was a jealous woman." Then the Prophet (Peace be upon him) said, "Sorrowful is the plight of the woman who makes her husband angry and happiness awaits her who makes him happy."

These conditions are a description of the sufferings (of the soul) to be borne in Barzakh. The Day of Judgment will be even more severe and harsh.)

I remarked to Haadi, "Haadi, we had decided to travel well away from the Valley of Punishment. How is it then that we are here? Have we lost our way?" He said, this is just the image of that Valley. Its hot smoke won't reach you."

We came out of the Land of Greed to enter the Land of Jealousy. In this there were numerous workshops. Dark men resembling Darkies were at work. The machinery was making such a deafening roar that one could not hear anything else. Dust and smoke had covered everything. The robot-like machines looked like huge giants and were made of a metal harder than steel, and these were moving all about the place. One of these approached us and stopped just in front. Suddenly Darky too flew in, looking like black smoke. I turned around and much to my dismay, could see no sign of Haadi anywhere. Darky said, "Want to see the machines at work? I bet you have never seen anything like this on Earth."

Though I wished to see the workshops in detail but since the suggestion came from Darky and since all his previous suggestions had landed me in trouble, I turned a deaf ear, and whipped my mount on. Reading the Surah-e-Falaq: "In the name of Allah, the Beneficent, the Merciful. Say, 'I seek refuge with the Lord of the dawn, From the evil of what he has created, From the evil of darkness when it overspreads. From the evil of malignant witchcraft, And from the evil of the envier when he envies."

Darky remarked, "Pity, Pity! You used to recite it on Earth, but never tried to put it in practice. Its not going to help you now."

Fear overcame me. I saw Darky approach the machine, and then he disappeared. I hoped that he had gone away, and was wondering where Haadi had gone when suddenly, Darky reappeared in the form of a fearful creature. My horse shied at the sight and went off-track, falling and throwing me down also just near the machine. I was hurt so badly that my body lost all feelings and I could not even get up. The dreadful fuming machines were approaching nearer and nearer, as if they were going to engulf me. Darky was screaming with laughter and saying, "Go on, read 'From the envier when he envies.' O Fool, name me one scholar and learned man who has been free of jealousy. You managed to escape from my previous traps and this has made my heart bleed. I'll see to it that you don't ever get out of this one." So saying, he caught me and tried to crush me.

His making fun of me angered me. Though I was weak I started to fight. But he was stronger and I could see that he was overpowering me. When I saw this involuntarily I started calling Hazrat Ali (A.S.) for help: "Ya Ali Madad". No sooner had I said this, all the machines which had been about to crush me, suddenly started a disorderly retreat and in the process crashed into each other, breaking into pieces Darky too tried to run away, but was crushed under the wheels of a giant roller. I said, "Wretched person, you were making fun of me. Now you are in the same boat that I was in. And nobody deserves it more then you do." This was my last encounter with Darky.

I managed to come back to the Main Road, which was the straight road and the correct path. It had only been Darky's mischief that my mount had gone astray.

But though back, I was too weak to go on or even get up.[38] Each and every joint ached, and I was extremely thirsty. It was hot and the atmosphere was full of the stink and smoke. Suddenly I saw Haadi running towards me. As he approached, he took out the portmanteau which contained Hazrat Ali's (A.S.) gift and from it took out a crystal-glass bottle. From it he poured out some clean, cool and sweet water which he offered to me. The water quenched my thirst and refreshed me physically, mentally and spiritually: "Verily, the righteous shall drink a cup tempered with camphor (Kafur)."

(38) Mistakes and sins (like jealousy for example) leave their effect on the soul and hinder man's natural progress on the straight path by weakening his resolve and intention.)

I saw that the entire ordeal had been too much for the mount. He suddenly fell down and died. Now I was left without a horse.

I picked up the backpack and put it on my back. Haadi picked up the portmanteau and we resumed our journey. The desert was larger than our Sahara Desert and had become dark and gloomy due to the constant emission of fumes by the machines. I noticed that men made of fireballs were tumbling out of the machines and falling down onto the ground just like cigarettes from a vending machine.

Haadi informed me that on Earth these people had been jealous of the faithful, due to one cause or another and used to show their jealousy by word or deed. Sorrowful fate awaited them inside these machines and due to constriction, this fire of jealousy came out from their within[39]. He quoted the tradition that Jealousy is like fire and 'It devours faith like fire devours wood.'

The route being dark, Haadi walked in front and I followed. I remarked to him, it seems to me that we are off track. Hazrat Ali's recommendation had been that I should not be troubled at all, but I have never before faced such troubles as these."

Haadi replied, "No, no, we are not lost. The fact is that hardly anybody is completely free of jealousy. Everybody experiences it. Through in varying degrees. Had you not had Hazrat Fatema Zehra's recommendation with you, your fate would have been no different from the people you saw. But remember, most of these unfortunate people after serving their time here will be released and will join the ranks of the blessed and happy ones."[39]

(39) (In this world our traits and feelings remain hidden in our heart; in the hereafter, however, they will become obvious even to others, embarrassing the sinner in front of all.)

As the air was hot and stuffy and my back was also troubling me, we walked fast in order to cross this land as soon as possible. The fear that Darky might still be alive and following me, urged me on yet faster. Rank and stinking sweat oozed from my body and wet my clothes. My ankles were dead tired and painful. It was with the utmost difficulty that, we managed to emerge from this land at last, and then we heaved a sigh of relief. A cool breeze started blowing and fountains of sweet water erupted.[40] The mountains and valleys were lush green. We sat down to rest by a fountain, I said, "Haadi, it seems that my Darky has been crushed under the wheels of the machines and has been killed." He replied, no, certainly not. He never dies. However, in this particular land he won't approach you because now we are quite far from the Valley of Barhoot. In front of us lies the land where people are being punished for their pride and arrogance. As you had managed to rid yourself of these traits in your lifetime, you will not be troubled there. From here the Valley of Peace is not far."

(40) After the soul has been cleansed of its vices and punished for its past sins, it will be able to enjoy the blessings and bounties. The Qur'an says, "Each of you will enter it (hell): Then we will send salvation for the God-fearing ones".)

As we went on the atmosphere kept on becoming pleasant. There was sweet scent in the air, luscious trees were in abundance and mountains covered with dense trees and waterfalls of sparkling water could be seen. In the mountain plains, numerous tents of fine white silk were visible.

# 10 Chapter

## SPRING IN VALLEY OF PEACE

Haadi said, "This is the city of 'Huma'. Here people stay in these tents." The pillars and pegs of these tents were of gold and the ropes were of silver. While we were still some distance away Haadi said, "Wait here, I'll go and find your place." I asked, What is this place called. The atmosphere here is so pleasant and peaceful I wish that we could stay here for a few days."

Haadi said, "This is the Valley of the Right and the Sacred Land and you will have to stay here for a few days. Then he opened the portmanteau and took out Hazrat Zehra's gift. Taking it he went towards a certain tent. My eyes followed him as he approached it, took out a piece of paper from his pocket and read it out aloud. The front flap of the tent was at once pulled open and some beautiful boys and girls came out. They rushed towards me, with Haadi following behind. Haadi took out another wallet from the portmanteau and told me, "Go to your tent with these attendants. Rest and wait for me. I'll have to go to Aasma to arrange accommodation for you. "I said 'Haadi, I am a stranger here without a single friend. Don't go away."

He said, "Its for your sake that I'm going and consider this to be your own country. Go to your tent. You will not be alone. You will find friends there. 'In the tents are beautiful maidens as yet untouched by humans or jinns.' (Surah-e-Rehman Verse 72)

Saying so, Haadi left. I came to my tent with the attendants respectfully hovering around me. A maiden was sitting inside on a divan. She stood up to greet me. After a while, a handsome lad came in. In his hands were a silver bowl and towels. He helped me wash my hands and face with rose-scented water.

Now when I caught a glimpse of myself in a mirror, I was surprised and pleased to see that I was no less beautiful than the maiden sitting beside me who had been gifted by Allah. "Men have authority over women" (Surah-e-Nisa Verse 34)

We sat down on the divan. I looked around and noticed that the tent was supported on five pillars, the central one being the tallest and firmest of all. It was gold plated and studded with rubies and emeralds.
Wishing to test the maiden sitting beside me, I asked her why there were five pillars in the tent.

She replied, "All tents in the Valley have five pillars. This is because Islam also has five pillars: Prayer, Fast, Hajj, Zakat and Khums, and Wilayat (love and friendship of the Ahle bait). The central one is of Wilayat and in fact it is supporting the whole tent. It is more important than others (as it helps to achieve all others)."[41]

I said, "I was under the impression that each of the pillars was symbolical for remembering each of the Panjtan (the immediate family of the Holy Prophet)."

She replied, "They are amongst the Usool i.e. Roots and this is the place for the Furoo or Branches and its connections and it is just the image of their Pure light. Prophethood and Vicegerancy, (Imamat) are both part of Usool.

(41) In Safeenatul Bahar, Muhaddis Qummi has quoted Imam Baqir (A.S.) as saying that Faith has five pillars, Prayer, Fast, Hajj, Zakat and Wilayat. The narrator Zarrara asked, which of these is the best? "Imam (A.S.) replied, "wilayat, because it is the very soul of the other deeds. "In the end he said if somebody spends his lifetime praying throughout the nights. And fasts in the days, spends all he has in the way of God. And performs pilgrimage every year but, he does not have an infallible Imam to follow, under whose guidance he has performed these deeds, he will not be rewarded for them and will not be given the rank of the faithful." (Because it is almost impossible to expect that without the guidance and teachings of the Imams (A.S.) we can perform deeds correctly with an understanding of the spirituality contained).

"The whole Universe and whatever it contains is in fact interrelated as if it has been prepared in one factory for a sole and common purpose. The difference, which is observed, is only due to difference of less with more, of roots with branches, of light with its rays. Man should try to reach these levels of depth in understanding and himself become a link in this chain of the Secret and Unseen. He would then become the center and core of all beings and hence the manifestation of the Name of God and hence God's Vicegerent.

"'Man by nature has this capability but he does not try to know his reality and instead wastes his time on Earth in material pursuits. Surahe-Asr says that, 'Albeit Man is in loss'. Elsewhere he is called 'Unjust, Ignorant' and 'Ignorant of Qadr (systems)."

I said, "May I inquire where you have studied? Your speech is certainly worth listening to."

She replied, "I have been educated in the Holy city of Madina and those green mountains and this invigorating atmosphere are much lower in status than it."

"The Holy Prophet (Peace be upon him) has said, 'I am the city of knowledge, and Ali (A.S.) is its gate.' I have been brought up by Hazrat Fatima (A.S.) who, like her father, is herself a city of knowledge and purity and she is the Blessed as the Night of Qadar and is better than a thousand cities of knowledge. It is almost as if Quran was revealed unto her. 'In it come for separation all wise commands most suits her. That, all matters are decided through her. She is the Olive Tree, which is 'neither to the east nor to the west, and its oil is close to being lit up though fire has not touched it'. She is 'Light upon Light', and it is Fatima (A.S.) on whom 'Angels and spirits come down in it, (night of Qadr) by the order of their Lord with all matters'."

She went on eulogizing Hazrat Fatima (A.S.), and I sat engrossed listening to her. Then she said, "This scroll which Haadi gave me was Hazrat Fatima's (A.S.). In it she has written that one of her sons is coming to me and that I should do everything I can for him as he is to be my owner and Lord. It seems that I'm the fruit and result of the seeds, which you had sown on earth. God has perfected your harvest and has given it to you in my form. As He says in Surah-e-Waqia Verse

"Have you seen that which you sow? Do you cause it to grow or do we?"

"I praise God and to him indeed belongs all praise and in the end praise is for Allah the Lord of all Universe."

After this a sumptuous variety of dishes and drinks was brought for us. The meal was too delicious to be described. There were bounties which, no human eye has ever seen, nor have ears heard of. After eating we reclined on the couch.

I said "It seems to me that you are not a permanent resident of this place."
She replied, "You are correct. I came here just to welcome you and I brought this tent and its possessions along with me. In fact all the tents that you see here were brought for welcoming its residents who are now staying in them. This is God's guestroom. When you proceed from here, I will go back to my own country'."

I said, "I feel like taking a walk in the garden and seeing the camps, the mountains and the valleys. And I suppose it's possible that I might even meet old relatives here."

She replied, "Of course you may. You are free here to do as you like. But just remember that before you enter any tent you should greet its inmates and take permission to enter. And for your information when I arrived, I noticed your eldest daughter's tent nearby. For your sake, I visited and befriended her. If you wish, we can visit her."

"Certainly, why not', said I. So we went towards her tent and as we approached it, I called out Salaam to her. Recognizing my voice, she rushed out, followed by a train of attendants. We greeted each other and thanked God for our reunion, and that in spite of our numerous sins, he had forgiven and blessed us. Then we went inside and sat down on a jewel-studded couch, facing each other, since this was better than sitting side by side.

I asked her what had befallen her on her journey and she replied, "The first station and the Land of Jealousy was quite difficult. It seems that most travelers face problems in these stages, though to varying extent. At certain times it seemed that my salvation was only due to your prayers for my welfare. I also wished and prayed for you. After that one of my sisters also had to undertake this journey. Then your time came and I prayed to God not to leave my mother and my brothers and sisters alone in the world."

"What befell your sister?"

"When she came here I saw that she was much higher in rank and station than I was and she told me that she did not have to face the various hardships that we have undergone. She saw the various lands but did not have any difficulty in crossing them."

"This is because she died young. You know that she was only eighteen years old when she died. That is why her journey was so much easier. We with our longer lives have managed to sin more."

Then I went for a walk in the woods. As I would approach a tree, its fruit laden branches would bend down towards me. The fruits were fresh and sweet and did not decrease in number regardless of how many I ate. Melodious voices rang out from the trees, inviting me to eat whatever I liked.

Then we returned towards my tent. From afar, I saw Haadi standing in the doorway waiting for me. I ran to greet him. He smiled and said, "You seem to be enjoying yourself here, visiting and sight seeing. But get ready for moving again. We are going to the city. The respected scholars and the faithful have received news of your arrival here and are waiting anxiously to meet you."

# 11 Chapter

## A VISIT TO HELL

I said "I'm prepared to leave, but Haadi, there's one thing which saddens me."

He said, "Sadness and in the Valley of Peace! I cannot believe it."

"You are right, but didn't you notice that Hazrat Abbas (A.S.) and Hazrat Ali Akbar (A.S.) are still in their battle-dress and blood stains still visible on Hazrat Ali Asghar's (A.S.) neck. I wish to avenge their deaths."

He replied, "But their enemies, the accursed beings, are in the Valley of Barhoot and it is the duty of the Twelfth Imam, the Imam Mehdi (A.S.) to avenge, which he shall, whenever he appears."

I said, "True, but I wish to go to the Valley of Barhoot and punish them with my own two hands."

"God has ordained two harsh and severe angels for this task. Do you consider yourself more capable than God and his angels?"

"No, no, of course not! Of course nobody is more severe

than God and his angels because he is the Ultimate Justice. No doubt he is Benevolent and Merciful, but he is also the Forceful and all Powerful. However, it was my desire to punish them personally."

"No doubt God will reward you for your feelings. But you should realize that the Faithful's luminance can cool down the fire of Hell. Are you willing that the heat should decrease for the period that you are there?"

He was right and so I said, "All right, but at least take me to some place from where I may be able to see them being punished."

When Haadi saw that I just would not be satisfied he left to present my request to the Holy Prophet (Peace be upon him), Hazrat Ali (A.S.) and Hazrat Fatima (A.S.). When they learnt about this, they prayed for my welfare and the Holy Prophet (Peace be upon him) said, "O Lord! We Ahl ul bayt are always content and satisfied with whatever your will is, because you only wish the best. We cannot dare object. However today one of your servants has come to your guesthouse where sorrow and sadness cannot enter, but he loves us so much that he wishes to see our enemies being punished and he will not be content until his desire is fulfilled. If you please, in order to satisfy him, allow him to see the Valley of Barhoot."

The Holy Prophet's (Peace be upon him) wish was granted. And it was ordered that I should be allowed to see the enemies of the Ahl ul bayt (A.S.) being punished, but that angels should accompany me, so that I would not be troubled at all in this journey. And the hot air would not harm me.

When I received this news, I was overjoyed and I started preparing for my journey along with a few of my friends.

We were accompanied with angels on all sides to protect us. Soon we approached a hill. When it was about a hundred steps ahead we saw that the eastern horizon was overcast with dark clouds and sparks of different shapes were emitting from them, as if they were made of fire and were bursting. We could hear the thunder from afar. As soon as the angels saw this, they involuntarily said, "There is no course of circumstances and no power except God's."

I asked, "What is the matter?"

The angels replied, "This is the Valley of Barhoot and these sparks, resembling arrows, spears, swords and cudgels are in fact the curses which the faithful send upon the enemies of the Ahl ul bayt and these are hitting their targets. But this is not the real punishment. The real punishment and wrath of God is being meted out in the plains of Barhoot. The plain is even warmer than the ironmonger's kiln. Snakes, scorpions and beasts made of fire are present there to continuously torture those accursed beings."

We climbed the hill. From here we could see that the fiery arrows would pass clean through the bodies which they entered. Each of the arrows, swords etc. passed through numerous people and if by chance any of the darts fell down it would get up again to continue hitting its target. If the people tried to escape, the arms would follow them until they would manage to strike. It seemed as if these arms and darts were conscious beings and also as if somebody was picking up the enemies bodily and throwing them down onto the ground here and there. It reminded me of the sight of mustard seeds popping about while being roasted. The enemies of the Ahl ul bayt (A.S.) were wailing away and their voices sounded like the whining and yelping of dogs. The sight gave me great pleasure and satisfaction. I sat down on the hill to enjoy the scene and since I had been informed that these arms were in fact the faithful's curses, I repeated the curse, which I used to read in Ziarat-e-Ashura.

"O God! Send down your curse on the first oppressor who did injustice to Mohammad (Peace be upon him) and his Progeny and to the last, who followed in his footsteps. O God, send down your curse on the wretched people who fought with Hussain (A.S.) and those who were with them and obeyed them and followed them in killing Hussain (A.S.). O God, send down your curse on all of them."

Then I said, "O god especially curse on my behalf the first oppressor, then the second, the third, and the fourth, always and forever."

"O God, curse Yazid son of Muawiyah, the fifth and curse Obaidullah son Ziyad and Omar son of Saad and Shimr and the families of Abu Sufyan, Ziyad and Marwan up to the Day of Judgment."

All the angels and friends accompanying me joined me in repeating these two curses again and again. The fiery arms increased ten fold in number and the atmosphere became dense and dark with dust. The punishment became much more severe. A spark would strike an enemy causing him to lump up in the air, where he would be struck by more darts from all directions. They were being tossed around like footballs, managing to land only after a length of time. On seeing this we continued cursing until our voices became hoarse and throats dry. By now the accursed people had been roasted alive, their skins were peeling, and their bodies had become pierced like sieves. They were wishing that they would die but here even death could not rescue them because here there was no death; only eternal wrath and punishment. On earth they had oppressed until death had freed the oppressed from their tyranny, but in the

Hereafter since death does not exist, the oppressors could not escape their eternal harsh fate. The Quran says: "The Hereafter is in, fact life" and "Whenever their skin will burn away, we will replace it with another."

Here we also observed two strange sights. One that amongst these people there were two men whom fire could not reach. Flames would leap towards them, but would be turned away by large fans thus keeping the two men safe. When I inquired, I was informed that one was Haatim of Taai, the other Nausherwan the Just. Being infidels, they had been sent to Hell but the generosity of one and the justice of the other kept its flames away from them, as generosity and justice both were God's favorite qualities and he does not let anybody's labor go waste or un-rewarded.

Secondly, I saw some people who though also present in Hell were out of reach of its flames and was also not troubled by its fiery darts. However though they were not being punished themselves, they were losing their wits just seeing others being punished. Their faces had gone white and they were completely bewildered and terrified. I was informed that these were friends of Ahl ul bayt and they used to hate the enemies of Ahl ul bayt but they had been neglectful of their prayers and fasts and other obligations and had also not avoided the forbidden deeds. They were also answerable to others. The Just could forgive disobedience and sins but could not overlook the rights due to other men. So they were sent to hell but their love of Ahl ul bayt became a shield, saving them from its fire. At the termination of their sentence, since they had been correct in their faith and beliefs, if God so willed, they would be freed from Hell and would enjoy God's blessings.

Seeing the fate of the enemies of Ahl ul bayt really gratified me and we resumed our journey saying, "O God, give them such a punishment from which even the dwellers of Hell would wish that they were freed."

# Chapter 12

## A SINCERE APPEAL

The original text ends here. The translation was not meant for scholars who can benefit from the book in its original form, but for the public so that they may read and benefit by taking stock of their deeds and actions and hopefully atoning, repenting and asking forgiveness, before death overcomes. God is Most Merciful and if anyone truly repents God is willing to forgive completely. In order to maintain interest, at places the text has been abridged, and lengthy references and philosophical discourse avoided. Certain sentences footnotes and explanations have been added to the original text by the translator.

The conditions of the Grave, the Lands of Lust, of Jealousy, of Greed and Avarice, Satan and the Satanic Twin (Darky) and his destructive activities, his inciting and misleading arguments wherever possible. The punishment meted out to the sinners for their wrong deeds, the fate of pride, and good deeds going waste due to certain sins, all these are occasions for awakening and contemplation. One should try to prepare and stock deeds for the future because death is inevitable and it closes the door of action forever. If we fail to do good for our selves it is indeed foolishness to expect that our children will act on our behalf after our death.

We can only expect those deeds, which we have managed to do, to come to our rescue and help, and cannot be certain of anything else.

My God help every body to atone and do good. All praise is for God.
Peace be upon Mohammad and his progeny.

# 13
Chapter

## SAFEGUARDS AGAINST DANGERS

Although the events after death have been described already and will prove to be an incentive towards preparing for the Hereafter, but as nobody can escape from this journey, I wish to list some occasions and practices narrated by reverend personalities which will help everybody in their preparations. Only those who are aware of the reality and facts about the Hereafter can inform us about this and these are Mohammad (PBUH) and his progeny who are the cause of the creation of the Universe. And the gist of their teachings is that if anybody has to undertake a journey, he should make preparations for it.

Therefore, daily before sleeping, Hazrat Ali used to announce from the mosque, "O People, get ready and make preparations for your journey of the Hereafter. May God have mercy on you. The proclaimer of death is announcing 'Take heed. Be prepared for departing; you will face numerous dangers there. (Nahjul Balagha)

The first of these is the time when one experiences the pangs of death. (Surah-Q verse 19). This is an extremely hard time. On one side there is the intensity of pain and illness, the tongue becomes mute and the body refuses to respond. On the other hand, the crying and wailing relatives. The thought of being separated from them forever. The grief of the children becoming orphans, separation from one's mate and life partner. And from wealth and otherworldly goods (in the collection of which one had spent his lifetime); the agony of death, combined with these hardships, and the thought of the forthcoming hardships to be faced after death. All cause this time to be painful beyond imagination. Sheikh Sudooq has quoted Imam Jafer-e-Sadiq as saying, "If anyone wishes to make the pangs of death easy and light, he should maintain good relations with his relatives and should be kind and gentle with his parents. One who behaves thusly will die easily and in his lifetime he will not be troubled with paucity and will on the contrary live happily." The Holy Prophet has recommended Sura-e-Yaseen and Sura-e-Wassaaff-aat and reading the dua 'La ilaha lila Allah Ul Haleem ul Kareem. La ilaha illala ul ali-ul azeem, subhanallah-eRabbi-ssamawat-e-wal arze, wa rabbil arzeen-as-sabhe, wa maa feehinna, wa maa baina-hunna wa Rabbul arshil azeem, wal hamdu-lillahe Rabbil a'lameen.(There is no power except God, the forbearing and gracious) to the end in the Qunoot as being beneficial for the time of death.[42]

(42) (Recommending of particular duas and surahs for particular objects is because of the special meanings contained in them, which if understood and taken to heart, have corrective influence upon man.)

Second occasion: Adeela Indul Maut (Satanic thought in death): This is the turning away from the Truth to the false and wrong at the time of death. This is because Satan approaches men at the time of their death creating and raising doubts in their minds to the extent that one's correct faith may be completely shaken; one may even become bereft of it and he may die an infidel or faithless. Tradition advice us that as safeguard one should be in the habit of recalling the Usool-e-Deen with its proof so that when he is reminded.

Of the Usool at his death bed, and in Talqeen, certainty of faith would prevail and doubts would cease. Dua-e-Adeela, present in Mafateeh-ulJinaan is also helpful and should be read at the deathbed. Reciting the tasbeeh of Hazrat Fatima, wearing Aqiq (cornelian) ring, reading Sura-eMaumenoon on Fridays, reading Bismillah... La Haula Wala... after Morning and Maghrib Prayers, are all beneficial.

Third occasion; Wehshat-e-Qabr (Fear and horror of the Grave): This is more severe, and fearful than the previous occasions. When the body is brought near the grave it should not be put into it at once. Since this is a very fearful time, it should rather be prepared for it by breaking the journey thrice (Manzil), because the spirit still retains interest in the body.

The Holy Prophet has said. "The most fearful time for the dead is their first night in the grave. Help your dead in this hour of need by giving charity on their behalf and by praying for them (Namaz-e-Wehshat)." In this prayer, in the first Rakaat one should read Ayat-ul-Kursi after Surae-Hamd and in the second after Sura-eHamd Sura-e-Oadr ten times. Alternatively, in the first Rakaat, Sura-e-Tawheed (Qul howa Allah) is read twice and in the second, Sura-e-Takaasur ten times.

Also beneficial is reading La Ilaha Illa Allah ul Malik ul Haqqul Mubeen (There is no power except God, the king, the right, the manifester) 100 times daily and reading Soora-e-Yaseen every night before sleeping.

Fourth occasion: Constriction in the Grave: This is also a

difficult time. The grave calls out every day I am the rest house of the travelers; I am a house of Horror and also of Respect. "For some, the grave will be a garden from amongst the gardens of Heaven and for others a pit from the pits of Hell. Imam Sadiq A.S. has said that nobody can escape this constriction, but there are practices which can prove helpful in this regard e.g. Hazrat Ali has said that reading Surah-e-Nisa every Friday will save one from constriction. One who makes a habit of reading Sura-eZukhruf will remain safe from the constriction and beasts in the grave. Imam Jafare-Sadiq A.S. has said that whoever dies between Thursday noon and Friday noon will be spared constriction. Imam Raza A.S. has informed that the habit of night prayers keeps one safe from constriction. The Holy Prophet has said that reciting Sura-e-Takaasur before sleeping helps to ward off constrictions. People buried in the sacred land of Najaf are also spared constriction.

Fifth occasion: The questioning of Munkir and Nakeer: Imam Jafar-eSadiq A.S. has said that one who does not believe that questioning will take place in the grave is not a true faithful. These questions have been mentioned already. Reading Talqeen twice before burial is completed is very beneficial but especially (and maybe only) if the person had these believes and thoughts in his lifetime.

Sixth occasion: Barzakh: Barzakh has been discussed already. It is a time of extreme helplessness. Deeds done for the dead and the benefits arising from one's previous deeds are the only useful things at this time.

Seventh occasion Day of Judgement: It is the harshest, severest and most fearful day. There are fifty stations in the Day of Judgement, each more difficult than the previous.

I hope that the readers of this book will pray for me.

# 14

Chapter

## Notes

(1) (Kitab-e-Manazil-e-Akhkirat by Mohaddise Oummi)
(2) (The punishment in the grave, the questioning of Munkir & Nakeer and the presence of snakes and scorpions in the grave is mentioned in numerous traditions. The details can be had from the books on Beliefs.
e.g. Sheikh Sudooq and Allama Majlisi may be referred to.)
(3) (According to traditions, the light of the Friendship of the Imams will help their friends in the difficult moments after death, as love
strengthens heart and resolve.)
(4) (This presence of mind and the ready and appropriate reply befits
the author who led a life of piousness. benevolence. lofty morals, in service of humanity, and in quest of knowledge about God. Those who lead such lives will enjoy similar conditions. But the ignorant, wordly, cruel and evil will be in difficulties. Therefore man should pay heed, repent and start doing good from now.)
(5) (It is necessary to know the beliefs and principles of Islam like the Unity of God, Divine Justice, Prophethood, Imamat and the Day of Judgement, through understanding and logical proof. In this case, Taqleed following a Marjaa or scholar is not permitted. It is not sufficient if one adopts these beliefs because his forefathers believed in them. Blind following in this manner will prove useless in the Hereafter. As Islam is a religion of logic and evidence, the

Muslim should strive to know the Beliefs and principles through logic and clear understanding of proofs.

If this is not done, then his beliefs cannot be considered to be free of doubt and he would consequently not qualify to stand amongst the true Muslims in the Hereafter. Faith is a state of the heart, but it is attained only when religion has been principles through logic. Otherwise, Islam obtained through mere following is not of lasting quality and does not provide the necessary incentive required to work for the Hereafter. However proper understanding of religion through logic and proofs will result in the height of awareness and knowledge, which in turn will prove to be an incentive for doing deeds for the Hereafter.

(6) (Here the author has embodied the love of Ahl ul bayt to show how this love will come to help in all situations. The famous tradition of the Holy Prophet says: "One who dies loving of the Progeny of Mohammed, dies a Martyr". Imam Mohammad Baqar stated to Abu Khalid kabuli. "O, Abu Khalid! By God, the love of Ahl ul bayt illuminates the heart of the faithful like the sun illuminates the day". Imam Shaafai says: "I firmly hold on to the rope (covenant) of Allah, as we have been commanded, and this is the love of Ahl ul bayt". But it should be pointed out that mere vows of love are not sufficient unless one's deeds are also in accordance. The eighth Imam, Raza (A.S.) said: "We do not have a permit to free any one from the flames of Hell. And our intercession cannot overcome Divine Justice. One who is obedient to Allah is our friend, and the one who is disobedient is our foe". This shows that a claim of love and friendship of Ahl ul bayt will hold only when backed with deeds, which are according to Ahl ul bayt's wishes and desires. Otherwise to continue leading a life bereft of good deeds and even indulge in evil and then to depend upon the love of Ahl ul bayt is to deceive oneself.)

(7) (Constriction in the grave and other punishments of the Barzakh, are the result of those sins which one has not repented for. It has nothing to do with correctness of one's faith. The possibility exists that a person though a true faithful commits certain mistakes or sins in his lifetime, and will have to bear the punishment for these in the Hereafter. Therefore man should only sin to an extent that he can bear to be punished for. Saad Ibne Maaz was one of the respected companions of the Holy Prophet. When he died, the Holy Prophet accompanied his funeral bare foot and without his cloak to show his grief. The Prophet himself laid Saad in the grave, prayed for him and said that Gabrail and Meekail along with a host of angels were present in the funeral. But when Saad's mother said, 'O Saad! You are indeed fortunate that the Holy Prophet has walked barefoot in your funeral and has lowered you in your grave, The Holy Prophet asked her to be quiet and said, You cannot prevent him from suffering the punishment of the grave. Saad did not treat his family members kindly and so is now suffering constriction.").

(8) (Allama Majlisi in his book Haqqul Yaqeen writes that the spirits came to visit their family weekly, monthly, or annually depending upon their rank. They arrive in the form of a bird, and sit on the wall of the house and watch. If the family members are happy and busy in good deeds, the spirit also becomes happy and if otherwise, the spirit becomes sad. On Thursday nights, these spirits arrive. An angel accompanies the spirits of the faithful. If the family members are in any kind of hardship, then the angel shields them from the spirit's view, that he may not be troubled by their plight.)

(9) (In Usool-e-kafi, Imam Sadiq is quoted as saying that in the west there is a beautiful garden, watered by the Furaat. The spirits of the faithful reside here. They recognize each other and visit each other. In the mornings they are free to fly out from here. In the East there is

another valley, this one in meant for the wicked and the sinners. Here the spirits are punished for their past deeds, their food is bitter and their water stinks. Probably this description refers to the Valley of Peace and the Valley of Barhoot.)

(10) (Traditions show that when Satan lost favor of Allah he was granted the wish that a child of his would be born whenever a human being was born, and he would remain the latter's constant companion even in Barzakh. His lob would be to mislead people. If the human being had overcome the Satanic commands and his own desires in the earthly life, then this twin would remain over powered in Barzakh and cause no harm. However, here he will cause problems and troubles to the extent that Man had sinned in his earthly life. As the Prophet had said "I too had this Satan but he embraced Islam on my hands."

The gist of this is that human being has his carnal and material desires from birth and no man is an exception. If he gives in to these and errs, he will subsequently regret, feel remorseful and consequently suffer. The successful one is he, who is so firm of mind that he always overpowers his desires. The ideal being was Holy Prophet (S.A.) who had completely vanquished and triumphed over desires.)

(11) When man has to confront the consequences of his actions, he wishes he had never committed them. But this repentance is often not serious enough to stop him from again falling in for temptations and desires.)

(12) This is in accordance with the philosophical argument, the gist of which is that people judge things in accordance with their own nature. A sinner does not see wrong or bad in sins and disobedience in fact finds pleasure and contentment in these. Whereas a righteous person would be horrified at these and just the thought of committing evil would sicken him.)

(13) Henceforth the author has used the word "Darky" instead of Satan or Twin, in order to make obvious the

darkness of Satanic incitements.)

(14) From the traditions of the Infallible we gather that faith is not a permanent resident of the faithful's heart. If he sins, faith leaves him to return only when he repents. As faith is divine and godly gilt it does not remain with the faithful if he indulges in sins. (e.g. lying, adultery, fraud, rivalry, etc.) and as faith departs he is engulfed in Darkness and Ignorance.

(15) (The author has hinted that whoever is proud and arrogant in the world, God will punish him in the Hereafter in such a way as break his pride and turn it to dust.)

(16) (Abu Jahl used to say, "I am the Respected and Elite. On the day of Judgement, he and others like him will be addressed 'O Respected and Elite, taste the punishment".)

(17) (If one practices denying his self and desires, after a while desires and whims will no longer trouble him.) But alertness and vigilance will have to be a constant practice.)

(18) (This tradition is believed universally by all Muslims. It means that, anyone who truly loves Ali, does not sin because naturally he tries to follow his ideal through thoughts and deed. Hence Ali's love acts as a shield against committing sins.

If one finds him to be proclaiming love for Ali but also committing sins, he should closely observe and question this love. As to whether there really is true love in his heart and if so, is it just for the name -ALI or whether it is for Ali's qualities, habits, life style, ideals, thoughts and deeds? Are all these acceptable to him and do these appeal to him, because "ALI" represents these and not merely a historical name.)

(19) (It is an accepted fact that the way to happiness and success lies in opposing the satanic incitements and desires.)

(20) (As said before, if satanic incitements and desires are constantly opposed, they gradually lose the power to misguide and doing good continuously further increases

one's eagerness and appetite for good deeds.)
(21) (Possibly (a) knowledge and (b) piety as they have served the purpose of a guiding stick and a shield in the world and so might take these farms in the hereafter.)
(22) (Spirits are sometimes able to visit their families, according to certain traditions).
(23) (When a person's mind attentively concentrates on another, it is possible that it causes the other to compulsively think of him.)
(24) (Praying sincerely for the dead can improve their lot as God may bless them through his mercy and forgiveness.)
(25) (There is a hint here of how carefully one should live in the world. Keeping tight rein on his desires, especially for women, because such pleasure is nowadays easily available. And if one is not extremely vigilant to restrict his desires to his wife, he is sure to indulge, to whatever little extent, in unlawful and forbidden pleasures for which he will have to suffer. And God forbid if, he should commit the extreme act, then for such people there is harsh punishment unless they sincerely repent and are forgiven by God.)
(26) (Being married and having lawful means for fulfilling one's natural and instinctive sexual desires helps man to a great extent to reject extramarital temptations.)
(27) (The Arabic word is used to order away dogs.)
(28) (Those who deviated from the path were those who had deviated on earth.)
(29) (Sins committed leave their impression on the mind, heart and spirit and spoil one's self and character.)
(30) (in this world too, one has to struggle and strive continuously against sins and desires and try continuously to improve oneself or else he falls stagnant and his qualities might rest and even recede. Leaving sins and bad habits, increasing religious knowledge and improving on one's deeds is a never-ending struggle.)
(31) (If one decides firmly to leave his wrong ways and

takes the right initiative, the rest becomes easy. God has promised that if one goes towards him a little bit, God will respond by coming forward a great deal more.)

(32) (If man conquers his desires then in God's eyes he has a higher rank than even angels.)

(33) (One gets carried away by success, (even if it is spiritual) and becomes heedless of the scheming of Satan.)

(34) (Hazrat Ali: "How lengthy is the journey (of the Hereafter) and how meager our store of provisions (that is, good deeds which would help there.)

(35) (The Holy Prophet once told his companions that whoever says "La ilaha illal'lah" (there is no power but God) once, the angels prepare a tree for him in Heaven. They remarked, 'In that case, by now we must be having a garden each'. He replied, 'Yes, but on the condition that you abstain from sins, like conceit because it destroys the trees.)

(36) The real value of worldly goods in the eyes at God and the Infallibles, In Nahjul Balagha, Hazrat Ali (A.S.) calls the world and its possessions "dead bodies."

(37) There is a famous tradition of the Holy Prophet (Peace be upon him) which describes almost similar conditions. This is quoted in the book 'Roahe Rehan' from the book 'Kaafi' quoting Hazrat Ali (A.S.) as saying that he and Hazrat Fatima (A.S.) once visited the Holy Prophet (Peace be upon him) and found him in tears. They asked him the cause and he replied, "O All the night that I went for Meraj (Ascension) I saw some women of my Ummah who were being so severely punished that I became concerned for them and started crying. l saw a woman who had been hung by her breasts. Then I saw a second woman who was eating her own flesh and a fire raged below her. A third woman was hanging by her tongue and boiling water was being poured down her throat. A fourth was bent double, hand and feet tied together, snakes and scorpions crawling all over her. A fifth was deaf, dumb and blind, enclosed in a cage of fire, her brains oozing out of holes in her skull. Her

body was breaking to pieces due to leprosy.
Another was hung by her feet, inside and over. Yet another woman's body was being shredded to pieces by scissors made of fire. One woman had a head of a pig and a body of a donkey and was being given several kinds of punishments. Another had the face of a dog, fire was entering her body from her behinds and coming out of her mouth and the angels were giving her a beating with iron rods."
Hazrat Fatima (A.S.) then inquired of her father (Peace be upon him) "Pray, tell me, what had these women done?" He (Peace be upon him) replied, "Listen, beloved one, she who was hanging by her breasts used to deny her husband his rightful pleasure. The one hanging by her feet used to go out of her house without her husband's permission. The one eating her own flesh used to beautify her and show her body to men other then her husband. The one who was tied hands and feet together, with snakes and scorpions on her, never used to care about the filthy and unclean, or 'Najaasat and was not careful about bathing regularly after menses, intercourse etc, thus taking her prayers lightly. The deaf, dumb and blind used to bear children through adultery but would claim they were her husband's. The one whose body was being cut by scissors made of fire never took care of her Hijab in front of Na-Mahrams (men other than those allowed to see her). The one whose body was being burned and who was eating her own intestines used to provide other women to men for sex. The one with the face of a pig and body of a donkey was backbiter and a liar. And the one with the face of a dog, with fire entering from her behinds and coming out of her face, was a jealous woman." Then the Prophet (Peace be upon him) said, "Sorrowful is the plight of the woman who makes her husband angry and happiness awaits her who makes him happy."
These conditions are descriptful of the sufferings (of the soul) to be borne in Barzakh. The Day of Judgement will be

even more severe and harsh.)

(38) Mistakes and sins (like jealousy for example) leave their effect on the soul and hinder man's natural progress on the straight path by weakening his resolve and intention.)

(39) (In this world our traits and feelings remain hidden in our heart; in the hereafter, however, they will become obvious even to others, embarrassing the sinner in front of all.)

(40) After the soul has been cleansed of its vices and punished for its past sins, it will be able to enjoy the blessings and bounties. The Qur'an says, "Each of you will enter it (hell): Then we will send salvation for the God-fearing ones".)

(41) In Safeenatul Bahar, Muhaddis Qummi has quoted Imam Baqir (A.S.) as saying that Faith has five pillars, Prayer, Fast, Hajj, Zakat and Wilayat. The narrator Zarrara asked, which of these is the best? "Imam (A.S.) replied, "wilayat, because it is the very soul of the other deeds. "In the end he said if somebody spends his lifetime praying throughout the nights. And fasts in the days, spends all he has in the way of God. And performs pilgrimage every year but, he does not have an infallible Imam to follow, under whose guidance he has performed these deeds, he will not be rewarded for them and will not be given the rank of the faithful." (Because it is almost impossible to expect that without the guidance and teachings of the Imams (A.S.) we can perform deeds correctly with an understanding of the spirituality contained).

(42) (Recommending of particular duas and surahs for particular objects is because of the special meanings contained in them, which if understood and taken to heart, have corrective influence upon man.)

Printed in Great Britain
by Amazon